What people ar

Shine On

One of the most gripping accounts of a near-death experience that I have read. And I say that having interviewed, since 1965, thousands of people who described such experiences. [His] story also evokes... a primal horror of being dragged under and run over by a train! I still remember the chill that went down my spine.
Dr. Raymond A. Moody, Jr., bestselling author of *Life After Life*

Wonderful... *Shine On* is a fascinating account of an extraordinary experience and I recommend everyone read this book to understand the true importance and power of NDEs.
Dr. Penny Sartori, author of *The Wisdom of Near-Death Experiences*

Amazing, Amazing, beautiful book. I absolutely loved it. David's miraculous and moving story reads like a novel that brings you to tears. He used his spiritual experience to truly look within and change the trajectory of his life... beautifully weaves together the importance of the intersection of psychology and spirituality.
Dr Amy Robbins, Licensed Clinical Psychologist and Host of Life, Death and The Space Between Podcast

Wow! Absolutely riveting! It's so powerful and compelling! So impressed by the quality of the writing and the great story, and how real and grounded David comes across.
Lisa Smartt, MA, author of *Words at the Threshold: What We Say as We're Nearing Death*

Shine On tells the story of David's amazing experiences in an astute and very readable way. I can thoroughly recommend it.
Dr. Melvyn J. Willin, Paramusicologist

What an achievement this book is, I loved it and couldn't put it down. Kept thinking of people I wanted to share it with.
Stella Webster, *International Remote Viewing Association* UK Trainer

Shine On

The Remarkable Story of How I Fell Under
a Speeding Train, Journeyed to the Afterlife,
and the Astonishing Proof I Brought Back
with Me

Foreword by Dr. Raymond A. Moody, Jr.

Shine On

The Remarkable Story of How I Fell Under
a Speeding Train, Journeyed to the Afterlife,
and the Astonishing Proof I Brought Back
with Me

Foreword by Dr. Raymond A. Moody, Jr.

David Ditchfield and J.S. Jones, PhD

BOOKS

Winchester, UK
Washington, USA

JOHN HUNT PUBLISHING

First published by O-Books, 2020
O-Books is an imprint of John Hunt Publishing Ltd., 3 East St., Alresford,
Hampshire SO24 9EE, UK
office@jhpbooks.com
www.johnhuntpublishing.com
www.o-books.com

For distributor details and how to order please visit the 'Ordering' section on our website.

ISBN: 978 1 78904 365 5
978 1 78904 366 2 (ebook)
Library of Congress Control Number: 2019938409

Design: Stuart Davies

UK: Printed and bound by CPI Group (UK) Ltd, Croydon, CR0 4YY
US: Printed and bound by Thomson-Shore, 7300 West Joy Road, Dexter, MI 48130

We operate a distinctive and ethical publishing philosophy in
all areas of our business, from our global network of authors to
production and worldwide distribution.

Contents

What is written here happened as I remembered it, over time and I recognize that these are my memories of the events described in this book. Some names and characteristics have been changed to ensure privacy and for the sake of clarity, some people in the book are composites, and some events have been compressed and some dialogue has been recreated. But throughout, I have done my best to make *Shine On* tell my story, just as it happened.

Book website:
www.shineonthestory.com

Foreword

David Ditchfield's *Shine On* is one of the most gripping accounts of a near-death experience that I have read. And I say that having interviewed, since 1965, thousands of people who described such experiences.

Mr. Ditchfield's fascinating report also sheds light on relationships between near-death experiences and inspiration in the creative arts. For his close call with death awakened a talent for music that led to astonishing performances and compositions and fame as a musician.

There have been other cases in which near-death experiences opened previously hidden ability in music or painting. Mr. Ditchfield's encounter is similar to that of Dr. Anthony Ciccoria, a professor of orthopedic surgery at New York University.

In 1996, Dr. Ciccoria left his body during a near-death experience when he was struck in the neck by lightning and suffered a cardiac arrest. After he was revived, he unaccountably developed an interest in the piano. Now, in addition to being a professor of orthopedic surgery, he is also an acclaimed concert pianist.

I have also met several award-winning and respected painters whose talent followed on the heels of their near-death experiences. Mr. Ditchfield's story also evokes what is, to me, and many others, a primal horror of being dragged under and run over by a train!

Freud described an early memory of being in his mother's arms as a train steamed into the station. Freud said he felt his mother unconsciously lean forward momentarily into the path of the train. I read Freud's story when I was sixteen years old, and I still remember the chill that went down my spine.

I am glad that Mr. Ditchfield survived his primal ordeal, and I hope to meet this fine man someday.

Dr. Raymond A. Moody, Jr., author of the bestselling *Life After Life*

Part I

The Unfriendly Universe

Chapter 1

Falling Slowly

You idiot. You bloody idiot.

I knew I shouldn't have let this happen. It was the middle of the night. We were both laying on my bed, fully clothed, in the dark. I was holding Anna in my arms, her chestnut brown hair lying across the pillow, her warm brown eyes still looking up at me as the hope inside them drained away. She looked so vulnerable, and I could tell she was trying hard not to cry and that made it all so much harder.

I wanted to tell her the truth, tell her how much I liked her. In fact, more than that. I'd really fallen for her. But I couldn't. It felt safer to keep her at arm's length, because with Anna, if we got involved, I'd have to be real. She was the type that would hold me to it and I just couldn't live up to that. Maybe once I would have tried. But not now. Not after everything that had happened.

"It's okay," she said, sighing, "you don't want to have a relationship with me, I get it."

She tried to sound matter-of-fact, but I could tell she was upset as she turned over and pressed her pale face into the pillow. I rolled onto my back, put my hands behind my head and stared up at the dark ceiling.

We were friends, nothing more. I had to remind myself of that.

"It's not you. It's me," I heard myself say.

"Your trouble is, you think too much," she said, turning back to face me.

"I can't help the way I am."

"Why don't you talk to—"

"I told you. I don't want to see a therapist."

"But it might—"

"Might what? You think by talking to someone, it's possible to be happy all the time, because I don't see you being happy all the time."

The words came out a little more aggressively than I'd intended.

"That's not what I'm saying," she argued back, but her voice had no fight in it now.

I hadn't meant to sound so cynical. I was just angry, mainly with myself. After all, this was all my fault. As soon as she'd offered to visit, I knew that the question of where she was going to sleep would take us into dangerous territory. It was less complicated when we both lived in London; she had her flat, I had mine.

I even told myself before she arrived, keep her at arm's length, don't get involved in that way. But as soon as she'd texted to say she wanted to come, I knew I was looking forward to seeing her again, and almost against my own will, a wave of longing reared up inside.

Over the past few weeks since leaving London, I'd missed her even more than I thought I would and from the moment she stepped off the train, the whole day had felt so easy, spending a couple of hours in the local coffee shop, listening to her talk as she filled me in on what had happened in her life recently, then feeling comfortable with companionable silence as we walked around the town together. Finally, dinner and an evening sat talking about anything and everything, just like old times.

It was when we came to sorting out the sleeping arrangements, that was when it happened. The moment of madness. I'd offered her my bed to sleep in and said I'd sleep on the floor. She was worried I'd be uncomfortable, but I told her I was a tough guy, and when I said that, we both laughed and that defused the awkwardness of the moment. A bit. But my heart started beating faster for some reason.

"I've got a sleeping bag, I'll be okay. I just need one of the pillows," I said.

"Here you go," she replied, a flicker of nervousness unintentionally revealed in her voice as she picked one up and handed it to me.

"Thanks."

"Goodnight then."

"Goodnight."

And that was the moment. Our hands briefly touched as I took the pillow off her and that was when I made the move. That was what the strange energy in the room was about.

A thought flashed into my mind, one I didn't want to have. *Don't do this. Don't.*

As this thought took hold, I started to feel like an electric current was running throughout my body underneath my skin, and I couldn't stand the tension of lying next to her any longer.

"What's the matter?" she asked, as I sat bolt upright and swung my legs off the bed.

"I can't do this. I'm sorry. I'll sleep on the floor."

And that was it. I got off the bed, threw a pillow down onto the floor, pulled out a sleeping bag from the bottom of the wardrobe, lay down, put my face into the pillow and shut my eyes to block everything out.

In the dark and silent charged atmosphere of the room, I could hear her breathing softly. Then I heard her turn over and sigh deeply. Was she crying?

After a while, she began to breathe more softly again, and my heart sank because I knew we had tomorrow morning to get through before she was due to get the afternoon train back to London. If only she'd bought an earlier train ticket.

What was she thinking? What the hell was I thinking, inviting her here? Unable to sleep, I rolled over onto my back and stared into the blackness for what seemed like hours, trying to ignore the hardness of the floor. The last thing I remembered was gazing out of the bedroom window at the starlit sky outside and hearing the sound of a fox, calling out somewhere in the distance.

Next morning, breakfast was awkward and quiet. The two of us tried to be polite with each other as we drank our coffee and she ate the food I cooked for her, but last night hung heavily in the air and it wasn't easy for either of us to feign any kind of lightness to the conversation.

But it wasn't just the uncomfortableness of last night that unsettled me. As I stood by the sink, washing up the breakfast dishes, quite suddenly, a chilly breeze seemed to run down my spine, bringing in its wake an overwhelming feeling of foreboding. I couldn't make sense of the feeling and shut the cutlery drawer a little too forcefully, as though to shake myself out of its strange cold grip.

Anna looked up from the magazine she was reading. Her eyes looked red and I could tell she'd been crying, probably when she was alone in the bathroom. Trouble was, now she was no longer Anna, my friend. After last night, she was something else, although I wasn't sure what. And I was now something else to her too.

"Sorry, a bit clumsy this morning," I said, secretly wishing it was time to leave for the station already.

Huntingdon train station was, from the outside, a typical Cambridge Victorian municipal brick building, its grand front entrance and north and southbound platforms all canopied under a new flat roof. A large poster in the ticket hall proudly listed the times of the half-hourly service to London King's Cross Station, a journey of just over an hour on weekdays and slightly longer at the weekend.

It was bitterly cold as we waited on the London-bound platform. The rail track glistened in the low, harsh winter sunlight, as though it was coated with frost. We both started stamping our feet to keep warm, sheltering from the cold wind by the footbridge of the station platform, near to where two station CCTV cameras were mounted.

I looked around to see what the time was. The digital station clock over the platform entrance displayed the time in hours and minutes. And if you looked really closely and could make out the figures in the glare of the harsh sunlight, seconds too.

Anna rubbed her hands together to keep them warm as we waited. There were only two other people on the long station platform, a man and a woman waiting for the same train. They were kissing and holding each other, as though saying goodbye, and I felt guilty when I saw Anna glance over at them.

If I was honest with myself, part of me couldn't wait for her to go so that I didn't have to feel so guilty, but another part of me wanted to tell her I'd made a stupid mistake, tell her she should stay, come back to the house so that we could climb into bed and hold onto each other and never let go. But I still couldn't bring myself to say it and I couldn't explain why.

Finally, a metallic glint appeared in the distance, the London-bound train moving towards us. Within a few seconds, all four carriages come into view as the front engine pounded down the track towards the station.

I looked over at Anna. She looked cold, her breath was freezing into little clouds of ice.

"You'll be warm soon."

"Good, I'm freezing," she replied. Watching the approaching train, I pulled the collar of my coat around my neck, glad that I'd worn it. It was my warmest coat, three-quarter length, high quality, thick sheepskin with five brown buttons down the front and an inner fur lining that went all the way down the sleeves. I was wearing a thick jumper underneath, so the coat wasn't easy to get on and off in a hurry, but I didn't mind; it was cold waiting on the station platform, I had no intention of taking it off until I got home again.

The big, dirty diesel engine and the massive, heavy metal wheels clunking on the track grew louder and louder as the train approached. Then, as it arrived in the station, the metal brakes screeched underneath as the train finally came to a standstill, followed by a small, violent jerk and a hiss along the entire length of the carriages as the brakes of the metal monster were applied.

"This one looks okay," I said, looking through the window of the nearest carriage, "there are empty seats in here."

The carriage had sets of double sliding doors at either end. We walked up to the nearest one. The button on the outside of the right-hand carriage door turned a bright flashing green color and I pushed it. The two doors slid open and Anna got onto the train. A few seconds later, I heard a beeping noise, a door closing warning alert.

I stepped back from the open doorway. Anna was stood inside the carriage, but I knew we still had a few seconds left before the doors automatically closed. Enough time for a few last words. But what was I going to say?

"Will you keep in touch? Let me know how things are going," I asked before I could stop myself.

"Of course I will," she replied, in an overly bright tone. But I knew she wouldn't. Not after last night.

My hand rested on the outside of the door as I leaned over the threshold to say one last goodbye, to look at her face one last time, because I already knew, I'd really miss her.

An urgent beeping noise indicated that the doors were about to close, so I took my hand away and shouted my last goodbye through the rapidly closing gap. Then both doors slammed together with a dull and heavy mechanical thud. At the same moment, I went to step back and realized something wasn't quite right. For some reason, I couldn't step back. And I couldn't figure it out. Something seemed to be stopping me.

I looked down.

The edge of my sheepskin coat was clamped between the two sliding doors that had just slammed together. Just the edge of it.

That was all.

For a second, I thought everything would be okay, so I told myself not to panic, otherwise I'd look stupid in front of Anna. I told myself it would be okay, because train doors automatically opened when something was trapped in them. I'd seen it happen many times on the London Underground. Any second now, the doors would slide open again.

Definitely.

They would.

Then I heard a noise that made the hairs on the back of my neck stand on end. The train engine was revving up. My heart started pounding as the station clock reached the timetabled departure time.

15.57:55... 56... 57.

After another second, the engine sound increased in pitch. Adrenaline took over. I grabbed a fistful of the coat fabric and started tugging at the trapped corner stuck between the clamped doors, but it was no good. I couldn't pull the coat fabric free.

Look for the door button. The door release button. It says 'press to open' above the button. Hit it. Open the doors that way. Hit it again. Do it!

15.58:03... 04... 05.

No matter how hard I hit the button, the doors stayed shut. The control button didn't work anymore. I had no idea that the door locks were controlled by the driver and that he'd disabled the control buttons on the outside of the carriages, now that he thought the train was clear and ready to depart. I just kept pounding the button in the hope that it would open the doors and couldn't understand why it didn't.

The next moment, I heard a new noise. The engine sound changed. It became even higher, more intense. That was the moment I knew the train was about to move and it felt like the air had suddenly frozen in my lungs.

Then, with a small jolt, the train wheels started inching

forward. One inch. Then a few inches. Then a few more. Then a foot. Then even more as the dirty metal wheels rolled over and over on the oily track. I could see the huge wheels through the tiny gap between the train and the platform, in the black and oily pit below. It was like looking down into hell.

Without even thinking, I began walking quickly because I had no choice; because if I didn't, I knew I'd be dragged under the train.

15.58:14... 15... 16.

Come on. Think. Just keep moving. That's it. Keep up. You'll be okay. Someone will do something.

15.58:30... 31... 33.

Then increasing acceleration underfoot, forcing me to start running.

Have to go faster now – don't trip up – you can do this – people – there – inside the carriage – maybe they can help.

Running faster now, I heard myself shout, "HHHHEEEEEEELLLLLLLPPPP."

I could feel the impact on my fist as I banged on the glass window of the carriage doors and I could see Anna standing there on the other side of the glass, and for a moment, we looked directly into each other's eyes, a look of absolute horror on her face.

15.58:37... 38... 39.

Pace picking up – have to – run now – harder to catch – breath – maybe someone – will see me – stop the train.

Then I remembered, the platform was empty except for the other man who'd been kissing the girl. He would be the last person to see me alive and I didn't even know his name. As I passed him, he began frantically shouting, "Take your jacket off, take it off. TAAAAKKKKKEEEE IT OFFFFFFFFF."

But it was no good and I knew I didn't have enough time to turn myself into a position where I could slip my arms out from the tight fur-lined sleeves in the last few seconds I had left before

I got dragged under. And I knew I was really in trouble now. I really was.

Through the glass, I could see Anna's mouth was open and she looked like she was screaming although I couldn't hear her as the engine noise was so loud. Some of the other passengers appeared at the doorway and I could see through the glass that they were trying to help, but there seemed to be lots of confusion and panic inside the carriage.

I couldn't tell who was doing what, but it looked like several people were trying to find the emergency stop button, and I could see it all and it all looked very confusing because everyone was panicking. Even though half a dozen people were frantically trying to help me, I could see that no one knew what to do.

And that was when I knew I was about to be pulled under the train.

This is it. I'm going to die.

Nine Months Earlier

Chapter 2

The Great Silence

The luminous face of the digital alarm clock said 4.24am as the voice on the bedside radio announced that in the next program Professor Brian McKay would discuss the latest findings in the search for alien life. Rubbing my eyes, I threw the quilt back, and without switching on the bedside light, got up and walked down the familiar dark hallway into the tiny bathroom.

As I peed, I could hear the professor talking, his vowels sufficiently ironed out so that there was no trace of his background revealed in his reassuring, melodious and unhurried radio-friendly voice.

"In 1974, the most powerful message ever broadcast into space was sent from the giant Arecibo Radio Telescope. The message was sent in the direction of a nearby galaxy called M31, 25,000 light years away on the edge of the Milky Way. This particular galaxy was picked because it was the closest one in the sky at the time and was the first ever attempt by humans to make contact with alien intelligent life. No one knows if there is anyone out there to hear it, all we can do is wait and hope for a reply."

Normally, the deep and calm, measured tone of his voice would have been a reassuring presence in the dark, but not tonight. Above the sink in the small bathroom was a mirror and I felt a prickling on the back of my neck as I turned to look. In it, I saw someone listening to the radio, wondering what lay ahead in his life. A ghostly face, its gloomy expression bleached amber yellow from the shaft of street light that came in through the frosted glass of the bathroom window from the lamppost outside.

I looked at the mirror more closely. The funny thing was, the reflection staring back didn't look like me at all. I recognized the family cheekbones and the hair, mousy brown, needing a comb. But it was the eyes that were different, dark circles weighed down underneath them. I leaned closer to the glass, trying to see what was wrong with them; I was sure they never looked like this before.

The cheap, badly-laid laminate flooring of the bathroom started to feel cold underfoot, so hardly aware that I'd walked back along the hallway, I found myself in the kitchen looking at the table. It was only just beginning to get light in the east, but I could still see the letter, exactly where I'd left it last night, laid out flat on the table top next to the torn envelope and the empty beer bottles.

Dear Sir

We are writing to advise you that your rent is overdue by the following amount:

Outstanding rent: £1445.

We would therefore request that you settle the outstanding balance immediately and ensure that all future monthly rental payments are made in full on or before the due date, in order to avoid eviction.

We also remind you that if you remain in arrears, this could result in court action being taken against you, the costs, for which, you would be liable.

If you would like to discuss this matter further or arrange a payment plan, please do not hesitate to contact the office at the above telephone number.

Yours sincerely,

Henry Harlston-Smythe

Rental Property Manager, North London Office, UK Division

There was no sound anywhere except for the lone, disembodied voice, still talking about the search for alien life. Exhaustion was kicking in and I was getting to the stage where my eyes were starting to feel gritty and my muscles twitchy with tiredness, so I walked along the dark hallway back into the bedroom, got back into bed, pulled the duvet up over my head and tried to fall asleep again.

A little while later, a car alarm went off somewhere nearby and the accompanying sound of traffic from the nearby Highgate Hill confirmed it was mid-morning. The gnawing, hollow sensation nagging away in my stomach meant I had no choice. I had to open my eyes and get out of bed. I could avoid my life no more.

The bedroom was cold, so I pulled on my blue jumper over my T-shirt and the one clean pair of jeans I could find, and went into the small, cramped kitchen. Needing coffee, I looked in the fridge in the hope that I might find some milk, but it was empty apart from an unopened bottle of beer, the last one left from the four-pack I'd picked up on the way home last night.

I reached in for the bottle. I knew it was far too early in the day to drink, but the idea of the cold, fresh bite of the beer was strong. Just one mouthful, I told myself. It wouldn't hurt. Once the beer hit the back of my throat, I knew I'd be able to numb myself to the fact that my debts were spiraling and there was nothing I could do about it.

Just when I'd got the bottle opener positioned under the serrated edge of the lid, my mobile phone text message alert sounded. The phone was lying on the kitchen worktop next to the fridge and I could read the message on the backlit screen from where I was stood.

How are you today? Janet x

I needed that beer so much, I didn't care what time of day it was, but getting a text message from my younger sister filled me with shame for wanting it so desperately. For a few seconds,

I stared at the bottle as an uncomfortable image came to mind. Me, slightly drunk, a bit too early in the day.

It's not that bad, I told myself, sighing heavily. Nothing like that. I just needed a bit of help when I felt under pressure and I was under pressure right now. It was the rent situation, that was all. If things got better, then I'd stop drinking, of course I would.

The image refused to go away, and a wave of self-loathing rose up inside, so I put the unopened bottle back in the fridge, slammed the fridge door shut, picked up the phone and texted her back.

I'm good, thanks. Just off out, so speak later x

When I first told Janet that I wanted to move to Highgate she said it wouldn't be easy and she was right. As she pointed out, it was one of the most expensive property areas in North London. She looked it up on Wikipedia and said it was all Georgian town houses with big gardens in tidy, residential streets, exclusive golf clubs and a posh bit at one end, Bishops Avenue, known locally as billionaires' row, where the mega-rich lived in huge, security-gated mansions.

Even when I showed her the advert for my flat on the property agency website, she still wasn't convinced. She said the flat looked run-down in the photos and although I didn't want to admit it at the time, it was. A one-bedroomed flat on the ground floor of a grim, three-story ex-council block, tucked away out of sight of the rest of the surrounding well-to-do area.

At the time I didn't care about the expensive rent, or the fact that the flat hadn't been redecorated in years. Instead, I felt brave and reckless, as though it was going to be a whole new chapter in my life when I moved to London. I imagined a life where who I was would finally make sense; I would finally fit in somewhere, as though some great transformation would happen, simply by living here.

How wrong I was. I didn't feel any different to how I did before, back at home. Things were still not going my way, only now I was a lot poorer and London could be brutal if you didn't earn enough.

You could try as hard as you like, do everything you could to earn enough money, but none of this altered the fact that unless you came from the right background, unless you were part of the right set with the right education, London was just too expensive to live in. I'd tried my best, even starting up my own treehouse business when nothing else paid enough, but even that had gone quiet lately.

People always did a double-take when I told them I built treehouses for a living. It wasn't exactly what I planned to do when I first moved to London, but there was a market for them in Highgate.

The local estate agents reckoned they added value to a property by providing extra play space for kids and, luckily for me, most of the people buying up the large Georgian villas in the area were professional types, accountants and lawyers who couldn't even knock a nail in straight, which is where I came in.

But now autumn was on the horizon, no one wanted to think about treehouses, so commissions had dried up. The only other option I had for earning money was trying to get cash-in-hand work on building sites.

Stifling a huge yawn, I closed my eyes and let my head sink down onto the table to rest on my crossed arms.

It's not your fault, I forced myself to acknowledge. *Just give it time. Things will get better.*

Just as I was on the verge of falling asleep, the mobile phone text message alert sounded again.

Do you want to come over for the weekend? Charlie cooking lunch & boys would love to see you. Janet x

I never thought I'd end up looking forward to homely dinners and watching family television in the St. Ives suburbs of Cambridgeshire with Janet and her husband Charlie. But now I did, even if I had to fake confidence about how things were going in my life, especially as Charlie was so successful in his career. Janet once said that Charlie thought I could have done more with my life and it was the truth, because it wasn't exactly what my family hoped for me either, me ending up like this.

It wasn't like I didn't try hard at school. In my own way, I did. But the teachers didn't understand dyslexia back then; in fact at that time, no one did. Everyone thought I was being lazy when I couldn't keep up with the rest of the class, and in the end, I was left to stare out of the classroom window while the other kids got on with their lessons. I'd learned to deal with the consequences ever since, avoiding any work that involved reading or writing, which is why the treehouse job seemed like a good option at the time.

My older brother Ian was the complete opposite to me. He won a scholarship to a good school, got French horn lessons from the music teacher and ended up studying music at university, the first in our family to get a degree. Dad worked in a factory all his life, so it was a big deal at the time, and my life sometimes felt like the failure by which his success was measured.

I reread Janet's text message. It wasn't a hard decision to make, a choice between a cold depressing flat in Highgate and a warm family home. It took me less than five minutes to get ready, and within the hour, I'd taken the Tube to King's Cross Station and caught the next train heading out on the East Coast railway line to Huntingdon station, the nearest one to Janet and Charlie's place, my ticket paid for by my ever-increasing overdraft.

Even though it was a weekend, the train was busy and the only empty seat I could find was one of four seats around a table. The opposite seats were taken by an elderly couple. The man was reading a newspaper and the woman was staring at the list of train stations on the route map above the carriage window.

I took off my jacket and sat next to the window, so that I could watch the London suburbs speeding past. After a couple of minutes, I had the feeling someone was watching me, so I turned my gaze back from the window and noticed the elderly woman sat opposite, staring straight at me.

"Excuse me, is this the right train for St. Ives?" she asked, leaning forward. "Only we can't see it on the list of stations, but the ticket man told us this was the right train to get."

"Yes, it is. Just get off at Huntingdon station and catch the number 23 bus to St. Ives. Takes around ten minutes."

"Thanks, love. Only we're going to see the medium, Julia Knight, she's doing a demonstration tonight in St. Ives and we wouldn't want to get off at the wrong station and miss it," she said in a conversational tone of voice.

I didn't respond so she spoke again.

"She's very well known, in the medium world, although she doesn't do it to be famous. She's what you call a bit of a hidden gem, just tries to help people. We think she's very good, don't we, George?"

The elderly, thin man sat next to her, George I guessed, nodded and went back to reading his newspaper as she picked her bag up from underneath her seat, pulled out a crumpled flyer and handed it to me.

THE ST. IVES SPIRITUALIST CHURCH
DEMONSTRATION OF MEDIUMSHIP
An evening with
JULIA KNIGHT, MEDIUM
7.30 pm

"So, what does a medium do exactly?" I knew I shouldn't have asked but I couldn't help myself, mild curiosity taking over.

"They get messages from people who have passed over," she replied matter-of-factly.

"Passed over?"

"Passed on. Died, dear."

"Oh."

"You should try it. You might even get a message yourself. We've never had one, even though we've seen her three times now, haven't we, George? She really is very good."

The man nodded again and continued reading his paper. I went to hand back the flyer, but she put her hand up to refuse.

"You keep it. I've got another one in my bag."

I folded the flyer up and put it in my jacket pocket. I wasn't sure why I did, but I did. I had no idea why she'd decided to invite me. Was she some kind of eccentric, harmless woman who talked to anyone she thought might listen? Or could she see me as I really was, someone whose life was spiraling towards catastrophe?

Whatever she was, I didn't want to spend the rest of the journey talking to her, so I thanked her for the flyer and made a point of shutting my eyes and turning my head back towards the window to pretend I wanted to sleep. That gave me time to think.

As I felt the rhythmic clackety-clack of the speeding train carriage and the bright, cold sunlight flashed in and out of the tall trees at the side of the track, I started toying with the idea of going. After all, what harm could it do? If this medium was as good as the woman said she was, I might even get a message about my future, maybe even a positive message. That would be worth going for, because right now, I really needed it.

That thought made me open my eyes, and when I saw my reflection staring back at me in the train window and my breath forming a small patch of mist on the greasy, smudged glass, a wave of curious optimism rose up inside.

Chapter 3

First Contact

Just as I had expected, Charlie was his usual skeptical self when I mentioned I was thinking of going.

"You can't be serious? A medium? Really?" he said, smirking. The look on his face as he read the crumpled flyer I'd just handed to him at the lunch table said it all and I went on the defensive.

"It's good to be open-minded about these things." But as soon as I'd said that, I knew it wasn't the best thing to say to someone like Charlie. He didn't do mystery. He needed to find a way to solve anything he didn't understand. That was why he was such a successful software programmer, and that was why I usually didn't try to outsmart him.

"Rubbish. Mediums can't predict the future or talk to the dead. No one can," he said, handing the flyer back.

"The woman on the train seemed pretty convinced she was good," I said, feeling a bit foolish in the full glare of Charlie's skepticism.

"It's just cold reading and generalized guesses that desperate people are desperate enough to believe. Mediums know that most people go to see them when they have money problems or health worries or relationship issues, and they know if they make vague enough statements, something's bound to stick. If people are desperate enough, they hear what they want to hear."

"If he wants to go, there's no harm in it," said Janet, shaking her head at Charlie. But even though she meant well, I felt a stab of shame and hoped it didn't show in my expression. He'd just neatly summed up all the reasons why I wanted to go, and part of me knew he was right. Of course it was all rubbish. Of course people who went to see mediums were desperate and gullible. But it was easy for him to say that, his life was on track. Mine wasn't.

I thought about it for the rest of the afternoon, but I couldn't figure out exactly why I wanted to go, I just knew I did. Maybe I wanted someone to tell me that things were going to get better in the future. After all, what harm could it do? At the very worst, I'd waste a couple of hours, but I had nothing else to do apart from watching television with Janet and the boys.

Whatever it was, by 7pm I was ready to leave, and I ignored the smug look on Charlie's face when I put my coat on to go.

"Bye, David. Hope you enjoy it," said Janet with an encouraging smile on her face as I walked out the front door to begin the short walk into St. Ives town center.

The Spiritualist Church wasn't actually a proper church building at all. When I finally found it, tucked away in a small Victorian passageway, it took me two walks along the passage to recognize that the green front door of the former Literary Institute Building was now the entrance to the St. Ives Spiritualist Church.

Inside the main hall, the seating was arranged in rows. Plain wooden seats facing a small stage at the front. A dark wooden bookcase stood against the back wall of the hall, its shelves filled with books.

On first glance, it looked like every seat in the hall was taken. I recognized the woman from the train waving excitedly in my direction from the other side of the room. Luckily, her row was full, but then I spotted a single empty seat on the second row. People muttered and moved their bags and coats to allow me to squeeze past, and just as I reached my seat, the lights in the hall dimmed, and a man and a woman walked onto the stage.

The man spoke first. He introduced himself as Ray, chair of the Spiritualist Church committee and organizer of tonight's event. Then he introduced the woman stood next to him. It was Julia Knight, the medium. She was middle-aged and smartly dressed in a plum-colored trouser suit. I wasn't sure what I was expecting, but I guess I just wasn't expecting her to look so normal.

Ray thanked everyone for coming and said how pleased they were to have such a talented medium performing this evening, and he hoped everyone who needed a message would get one. Then he left her alone on the stage.

She walked to the center of the stage and addressed the audience in a clear, confident voice. She said that the purpose of her mediumship ability was to provide proof that life continued on after death. She said that the proof she offered came in the form of messages from those in the spirit world, meant for specific people in the audience. She said that her job as a medium was to try to identify the people in the audience that the messages were meant for, as these messages were meant to help us. Then she fell silent.

At first, she didn't say anything, she just stood still, staring ahead at nothing in particular. She looked like she was listening to someone stood next to her. Only there was no one. She nodded her head and muttered something under her breath, and then nodded again. And then she started the demonstration.

"I have a message for the woman in the pink sweatshirt. Yes, you. I have your grandfather here. He says his name is George. He wants to know why you were looking at his medals before you came here tonight?"

I heard a gasp, then, "Oh my God," and like everyone else in the room, spun around to see who had responded.

"Can you take this?" Julia asked a woman sat near the back, wearing a pink sweatshirt.

"Yes, yes I can. I was looking at Granddad's medals earlier today. I can't believe it. He passed last year."

"He says he passed over quickly. Something to do with his heart."

"Yes, it was. Heart attack."

"He says not to worry. He didn't feel anything, it all happened

26

too quickly. He's very happy over on the other side. He says he's with Elsie now. Does that name mean anything to you?"

With that, the woman started crying. "It's my grandmother. She passed ten years ago. Granddad never got over it."

"They are together now and very happy. He says you shouldn't worry so much about your son. He says your son will get back on the straight and narrow. It's just a blip. That's the word he's using. Blip. He's giving me the name Peter. No, it's Phil. Does the name Phil mean anything to you?"

"Yes, yes it does. My son is called Phillip. I can take that."

"He says your husband is worried about his health too. His lungs. He gets short of breath sometimes."

"Yes, he's worried it's something serious."

"Your granddad says not to worry. It isn't. But he needs to slow down a bit, make more time for himself. But he says you have been worried too. A bit down recently. Can you take that?"

"Yes."

"He says you shouldn't worry. The business will be okay. You'll struggle to make ends meet for a while, but things will turn out okay. I'm getting overseas. He is saying new opportunities will come from overseas. Germany? No, not Germany, it's Holland. That's it. Holland, I'm seeing tulips. Definitely Holland. Can you take any of this?"

"Yes, yes I can. I import hair accessories. I'm talking to a new supplier in Amsterdam. Oh my God. Is it really Granddad?"

"He's here, but I'm losing him. He's going now. Sometimes it's hard for them to keep the connection open. I'm sorry. I'm losing him, but he sends all his love and he wants you to know that he watches over you, always."

"Thank you, thank you," said the woman, still crying. "Thank you so much."

And so it went on. The medium would point to someone, ask them to take a name, and I had to admit, the old woman on the train was right. The level of detail in the messages was convincing, not just general guesses, at least that was what the audience responses suggested. I wondered how Charlie would explain all this away if he'd seen it firsthand.

Then, quite unexpectedly, she came to me.

About twenty minutes into the demonstration, I was suddenly overcome with the strangest feeling that she was about to focus on me, and right at that moment, she suddenly turned and pointed in my direction.

"I have a message for you in the blue jumper. Yes, you, on the second row."

I looked around at the people nearby. I was definitely the only one wearing a blue jumper. The people in the front row turned around to look at me and so did the people either side of me. Then I felt the strangest sensation, as though I'd been taken out of time, as though the medium and I had suddenly left the cozy municipal surroundings of the church hall and were somewhere else, some other place, just the two of us, standing alone.

What she said next was unlike any of the messages she had offered to everyone else. This one wasn't a message from a long-lost relative coming back to offer consolation. It was short and to the point, and delivered in a loud, clear voice. A different kind of voice entirely, so strange, so powerful, that made the hairs on the back of my neck stand on end as she spoke the words.

"Your life is going to change dramatically."

Transfixed and now unaware of my surroundings, my focus was entirely on her as she spoke again.

"They are telling me. It's going to be a big change."

"What kind of change?" I said, my voice sounding strangely thin in the electric silence of the room.

"They are not saying. But know this. They are trying so hard to help you; they want so much to be known by you. You are being cared for, led, embraced and carried, more than you can possibly know. Beyond anything you can imagine. It's only your mind that can stop you experiencing this in your heart when the time comes."

She stopped speaking and just stared at me. By this point, the silence in the room was deafening, the kind of intensity where you could almost hear the air itself, crackling with expectation. It was hard to find any power in my voice to speak as my mouth was suddenly so dry.

"But what is this big change?" I didn't have a chance to finish what I wanted to say. She cut in again, now pacing across the stage.

"They are not telling me. They're not telling me in what way it is going to change. But they are saying, be ready. It will be big. Very big. And that is all they are saying."

She stopped dead in her tracks, and I felt like my breath had frozen inside and I was still a million miles away from the municipal hall and the plastic chairs and rapt attention of everyone around me.

Then she closed her eyes, inhaled deeply, let out a loud sigh, and when she did, it was as though a strange spell had been broken and I was back in my body again.

"I'm sorry," she said, sounding exhausted all of a sudden. "I'm not getting any more. I've lost the connection."

And just like that, it was over.

After a few seconds, she seemed to go back to her previous style of delivery and started working with a man on the fourth row who had lost his cat. I didn't know what to think and my heart was still racing, but at least everyone turned to look at him now and I had a moment's privacy away from their stares to go over the exchange in my mind, to pore over the medium's words.

"Your life is going to change dramatically... and they are trying so hard to help you."

And even though I had no proof that it was based on anything solid or real, an odd sense of cheerfulness rose up inside me, to wrestle my rational side for control of the truth, to claim its foothold on the reality of what my future might hold.

It was as though a voice was whispering somewhere deep inside, "Come this way and don't be afraid," and I felt so excited at the prospect that things might finally get better that I found myself suddenly beaming as I wondered what the big change I was heading for could possibly be.

Chapter 4

If I Knew You, Would I Want You

I felt my mobile vibrate in my pocket. It was a text message from my new girlfriend, Emily.

Had shitty day at work. Bring wine when u come

You can't afford this, I thought, sliding my debit card into the bank card machine as the shop assistant put the bottle of Santenay Burgundy, Emily's favorite, into a carrier bag. For a few seconds, I froze inside, hoping the sale would go through and I hadn't reached the overdraft limit on my account. Finally, the machine displayed its message that the transaction had been approved, and I felt a visceral sigh of relief, as though I'd got away with it one more time.

But there was no need to remind myself of that, no need to think about the fact that I was now relying solely on cash-in-hand manual labor work and my rent was falling even further behind, especially not when Emily was from such a wealthy background, the extent of which I only realized the first time I went around to her flat.

She rented a plush, first-floor, one-bedroomed flat in a large Georgian villa on Templars Avenue, just off the Highgate Road. Visiting her flat was like visiting a parallel universe, one that was expensively luxurious, with everything a muted shade of cream or natural wood. It was a world where sunlight streamed in all day through huge sash windows and the warm underfloor heating was always on.

She never cooked, so the kitchen was unused. Its shining dark granite worktops were clear apart from the top-of-the-range microwave sat in the corner. The mirrored bathroom and plush, immaculate sitting room chairs, all arranged round a large glass coffee table to face the huge flat-screen television mounted on the wall over the granite fireplace recess, reminded me of a hotel. In fact, her expensive makeup and toiletries, scattered over the granite vanity unit in the bathroom, and the large pile of magazines, take-away menus and cab receipts on the coffee table were the only clues that someone actually lived here full-time. And by now, I knew enough about the rental market in this area to know that the weekly rental for this flat probably cost double of what mine did for a month, which also explained why Emily had certain lifestyle expectations that became apparent the very first time we met...

"You build treehouses for a living," she said, as we sat drinking coffee on our first date, her mouth thinning a little at this news, as though this occupation failed to meet some invisible standard of social acceptability that her world was ordered by.

"Yes," I replied, making a mental note not to mention the manual labor work, as she looked at me with what I was afraid was slight disappointment now. It wasn't surprising; after all, I could picture the type of privileged world she came from. I'd seen it with my wealthier treehouse customers.

But it didn't matter. The thrill of shock that she'd agreed to have coffee with me, after we'd bumped into each other in a cafe in Hampstead, had overpowered the doubt that said the differences between us were too great.

It's fate, I told myself, convinced that destiny had played a hand in this meeting and the medium's prophecy had materialized in front of my eyes, in the shape of the beautiful, haughty, ambitious Emily.

It's the big change. It has to be.

"And then I did a degree in the history of art," Emily continued, focusing the conversation away from the dangerous topic of my lack of income, back to the safety of her life, "but couldn't get a job in a gallery. Then a family friend heard about a job in Beat XM record company and that's where I am now, PA to the managing director, Adam. I'm not that interested in the music industry to be honest, but the job does have its perks. I get to go to all the major awards ceremonies and meet a lot of famous musicians, although most of them are absolute yobs, I have to say."

That was the moment I should have told her that when I was younger, I dreamt about being one of those successful yobs, spending my time touring the world, playing brilliant guitar riffs from my string of hit albums. But I didn't.

Memories of sitting in the back of a speeding Transit van flashed into my mind, hurtling down yet another motorway, sat in amongst the guitar and drum cases, feeling exhausted and sweaty after yet another gig in a smoke-filled bar, trying to get enough sleep till the next gig, the next support slot on someone else's tour, always hoping that our luck would change, that that elusive break might finally happen.

Once, I was proud of all this, but now, in front of Emily, it felt a bit childish and small. After all, she was someone who was clearly mixing with the kind of musicians who'd managed to succeed on a really big scale and an instinct told me she wouldn't particularly respect the failed ambition of unrealized dreams. Not when she seemed to respect her boss Adam so much.

"And then he ended up as managing director of his own record company. Of course, his family connections helped, but it's still very impressive," she went on.

As she told me more and more about him, I continued to listen, nodding in the right places, but somewhere inside, I started to tense up as a nagging idea took hold.

She fancies him.

In a deliberate attempt to put that thought out of my mind, I forced myself to think of something else and a different idea of Emily formed in my imagination. One where she was stood by my side as I introduced her to friends and family. Their expressions of pleasant surprise... David's done well for himself... Her presence confirming to everyone that things were on track in my life after all. She felt like a glittering prize and I couldn't believe my luck. I really couldn't.

Unfortunately, my friends Matt and Jimmy thought the total opposite, as I found out when I met them at the local bar that same evening. They both grew up on a housing estate in nearby Camden and this had been their bar for years. They always sat at the same table in the corner and they played in the local darts team, which they were proud to announce was still a proper local's team owing to the place not becoming "bloody upmarket" like the rest of Highgate and Camden.

Matt was a bricklayer and took great pride in the fact that he had a Diploma in Trowel Occupations. Jimmy was a carpenter and proudly declared he had a Foundation Diploma in Carpentry. They knew I had no qualifications whatsoever but whenever a job they were working on had an opening for cash-in-hand casual labor, they always gave me a shout. They were good like that.

After buying myself a beer at the bar, I headed over to their table and sat down. Matt and Jimmy were already a beer ahead and were both eating crisps. At first, they both looked thoroughly impressed by the news that I'd had a date and said so too, but after telling them more about Emily, their expressions changed and they didn't react as I'd imagined. On the contrary, Jimmy frowned slightly, and Matt spelt it out as he saw it.

"Rich girl. Poor guy. Not good," he said, carefully flattening out his empty crisp packet on the table top. "Never works out."

"What do you mean?"

"How you gonna hold yer head up in front of her if you don't earn as much as she does?" Matt replied, as though this was the most obvious thing in the world.

"He's right," agreed Jimmy. "You could get hurt if you're not careful."

"She's not like that," I said defensively, but I was secretly disappointed by their reaction. It wasn't what I expected. So what if there were big differences in our incomes, our lifestyles? Surely if we liked each other enough, we could overcome it?

It was the first time I could remember that the three of us had ever disagreed like this, and feeling annoyed, I downed the rest of my beer and headed towards the bar to buy another round of drinks. After that, nothing more was said on the matter.

My second date with Emily took place in a crowded, upmarket Hampstead wine bar where she'd arranged to meet up with some of her record company colleagues. I'd never been to this part of Hampstead before with its tree-lined streets and immaculate Georgian buildings, and I could tell from the sleek exterior of the wine bar that it would be full of people like my treehouse customers. Matt and Jimmy would have hated this place.

The bar was obviously popular as it was crowded, but I eventually spotted Emily across the loud, packed room, sat at a table in the corner with a group of people. I made my way over through the braying, jabbering crowd, and after the preliminaries of ordering more drinks and being briefly introduced to everyone, I sat down at the end of the table trying my best to fit in. Thankfully, her boss Adam wasn't there. I overheard someone say he was in New York. That was the only saving grace of the entire evening.

I liked to think that I'd developed a tougher skin since moving to London, but in reality, I clearly hadn't. Unable to join in with most of the conversation due to the noise of the crowd, for the rest of the evening I just sat there, sipping my beer and trying not to look too left out as Emily was engrossed in various conversations. Everyone in the group seemed to have the same clipped vowels and expensive-looking clothes and a certain dismissive attitude about large swathes of the population that only people from a certain class feel entitled to have.

We stayed until closing time, and by then, I'd drunk enough

to mostly block out the cautious, slightly critical expressions on their faces. The minute they caught my accent, saw my clothes, it was as though a whole social background had been signposted above my head.

I collapsed into bed an hour later after walking home through the deserted Hampstead and Highgate streets, feeling aggrieved at how the evening had gone and irritated, mainly with myself. Awkward moments from the evening kept surfacing, an unspoken pressure from Emily to pretend that I was enjoying the raucous laughter, the snobbish anecdotes, the in-jokes about people from her workplace, even if I had no idea what anyone was talking about.

Pulling the duvet up over my head, I resolved that I wouldn't sell myself out like that again, pretend to like people who didn't like me. But as much as I didn't want it to, another, more insistent thought took hold and kept me awake for the rest of the night.

You want to be accepted by them. Admit it.

From then on, we only met up at her place in the evenings and quickly got into a routine of staying in, drinking a bottle of wine and watching television till bedtime. As she worked regular office hours, it seemed easier to go around after she'd finished work and leave first thing in the morning. But as time went on, I couldn't shake off a sneaking suspicion that this arrangement was because she'd decided to avoid the uncomfortableness of introducing me to any more of her friends. She certainly didn't want to meet any of mine. We'd even had our first row about it, but she denied it when I asked if this was the case.

This ought to have been a warning, but I was so wrapped up in trying to make things work with her that I deliberately put it out of my mind or tried to imagine a future where we'd somehow make new friends together.

For a while, it almost worked, until the night we had the uncomfortable conversation that began the dismantling of everything. That was the night I discovered that my instincts about her boss Adam were right, their working relationship had been far more complicated than she'd initially revealed.

The truth came out when she'd been telling me an anecdote about him, about how he'd managed to sign a hot new band that every other record company had been chasing. As she was talking, the tone of her voice changed and an expression I'd never noticed before flashed across her face. It was one of admiration. Respect. Longing. That was when I asked her, point-blank, if she fancied him. I couldn't stop myself, I had to know.

The unexpected question had a dramatic effect, her eyes flashed with surprise, then guilt, before she quickly looked away to compose herself again. But it was too late and she knew it. I'd seen enough to know the truth.

It turned out that they'd been having a relationship for ages and had only recently split up. She insisted it was a few weeks before she met me, but the barely-concealed hurt and anger in her voice as she admitted this betrayed a rawness about him that suggested things hadn't yet healed, even though she obviously thought she'd described it in a casual, dismissive way.

"Honestly, it was over before we met. Anyway, I don't want to talk about it anymore."

The knot in my chest felt like it tightened in the charged silence that followed for the rest of the evening, and it was only when I escaped into the bathroom to get ready for bed that I could allow myself to slump momentarily, sitting on the edge of the bath, holding my head in my hands. I knew enough about Emily by now to know that I mustn't look weak or vulnerable in front of her, she wouldn't respect that.

But the thought of the two of them together...

Don't even think about it.

The uneasy feeling continued even after we'd climbed into bed, even though Emily kept saying I should forget she ever mentioned it.

"Fancy going away next month?" she said, changing the

subject abruptly, as we lay in the dark, neither of us asleep yet, even though we'd put the bedroom light out twenty minutes earlier. "There's an all-inclusive deal to Antigua on one of the travel websites. One-week, full board in a four-star hotel, £1200 per person, including flights."

"You want to go on holiday?" I asked, completely thrown by this unexpected change of topic.

"Yes," she said, the resolution in her tone of voice revealed even more starkly in the darkness. "I've got annual leave to use up."

Does she have any idea how little money I've got, I wondered? After our first date, she'd ignored this inconvenient truth by not asking me any further questions about my work. But now she was suddenly expecting me to find money. A lot of it. Was she testing me?

"What do you think?" she pressed again in a tone that wasn't really a question. "Shall I book it?"

I had to say something.

"Maybe in a few months I could—"

"I really want this holiday," she cut in, the frustration clearly evident in her voice. "Things are really stressful at work. Can't you find the money somewhere?"

This was the moment I should have told her the truth that we had both so carefully avoided till now. That I hadn't had a treehouse commission in ages, and I was surviving on nothing more than my overdraft and cash-in-hand manual labor work. That I had no qualifications. I had no money, but I wanted a chance to make good, to prove myself, if she'd stick by me and believe in me.

But I didn't, because the conversation about Adam had left me reeling. And that was probably why I made the huge mistake. I knew it the moment I answered her, when the words left my mouth.

"Okay. Leave it with me. I'll see what I can do."

The next afternoon, I sat for a while on one of the park benches that lined the meandering gravel path that weaved its way amongst the monumental gravestones of Highgate Cemetery. The East Cemetery had become a regular place to kill time before heading round to Emily's flat when I didn't have any work. I liked the quietness and peace of the place.

The huge granite head of Karl Marx, his implacable expression framed by waves of grey granite hair and beard, gazed serenely from his grey marble plinth as I sat on the bench below, wondering yet again where I could get my hands on enough money to afford Emily's holiday.

I hadn't slept much last night, so I closed my eyes and rubbed my throbbing forehead as thoughts about money were intercut with replays of last night's conversation about Adam. As I went over and over it in my mind, I couldn't escape a nagging feeling that said I'd somehow, somewhere made a terrible mistake and now I was out of my depth. Exhausted and tired from lack of sleep, I could feel myself about to momentarily drift off when my mobile phone rang.

A well-spoken, confident voice asked if I was the person who'd built a treehouse in nearby Makepeace Avenue last year. I said I was. He explained he was looking for someone to build a log cabin in the large garden of a new property he and his wife had just bought in Corringham Road, near to Hampstead Golf Club, and the people in Makepeace Avenue had recommended me and passed on my number.

It all sounded promising. He said he worked in finance, which meant they had plenty of money and they were keen to press ahead with a quote as quickly as possible. A full-sized cabin was considerably bigger than anything I'd ever attempted to build before, but I knew I was capable of doing it and the potential profit margin would be huge compared to a basic treehouse. In fact, a job this size and scale could bring in enough money to pay off my rent arrears and pay for the holiday.

Everything would get better, I told myself, just so long as this job fell into place.

Two days later, I went to the house on Corringham Road and after I'd done the site inspection, costed out the materials and put together a quote, to my surprise, they agreed to everything. All I needed now was to get them to make a down payment, then the job was in the bag.

The couple agreed to hand over a deposit on the following Monday afternoon at 3pm. I was to go around to their house in person to pick it up. Then I'd have some money coming in and everything would be okay. That was what I told myself. It would all be okay.

On Saturday morning, I looked across at Emily as she lay in bed, reading a magazine. She hadn't mentioned Adam or the holiday since, and I hadn't mentioned the log cabin job either. I wanted to keep it as a surprise until everything was confirmed.

Lying with my hands behind my head, I enjoyed imagining the scene on Monday evening when I'd turn up at her flat and announce that we should book the holiday after all. It was a good scene, and when it played out in my imagination, I looked stronger, more confident than I had of late. The worries about Adam temporarily put on hold, diverted by the promise of a sunshine holiday together and money to pay off some of my debts.

Just then, her mobile bleeped. She put down the magazine, picked up the phone, read the message and typed something in response.

"We've been invited to dinner at Adam's," she said as she was busy texting.

"Your boss Adam?"

"Yes. You said you wanted to meet more of my friends. He's invited us over to dinner this evening. It's a small charity thing. It'll be casual so no need to wear a suit, but keep it smart casual, okay."

And with that, she got out of bed and went into the bathroom to shower. The magazine slipped off the duvet where she'd thrown it and landed on the floor with a dull thud.

Chapter 5

The Casual-Smart Dinner Party

By 5pm, I'd tried on three pairs of jeans, all the clean T-shirts and work shirts in my drawer plus three sweatshirts and one jumper. I only had one smart shirt, a dark blue brushed cotton one that Charlie had given me. He was bigger than me so the shirt didn't fit that well. But it looked better than anything else, so in the end, I decided to wear that one with my dark blue jeans.

Then I got changed again.

I decided to wear my slightly faded jeans, a clean T-shirt and the blue jumper I'd worn to the medium demonstration, as I now considered it to be my lucky jumper. Fifteen minutes later, I got changed again.

In the end, I put Charlie's shirt back on with a white T-shirt underneath, the dark blue jeans and black trainers. Then it was just the socks that were a problem. I needed dark socks, but the only clean pair I could find had a large hole at the tip, which meant my big toe poked out when I put them on, but they would have to do.

I checked my watch and looked in the mirror one last time. I had a bad feeling about the whole night. I didn't feel right at all, not one bit.

At six o'clock I arrived at Emily's flat. I had £45 in cash in my pocket, the last of my cash-in-hand pay from a recent building site job.

"Wow, you look lovely," I said, as she opened the door. And she did. For a casual smart dinner party, she'd obviously made a really big effort. Her hair and makeup were perfect, and she was wearing an expensive-looking dark blue, sleeveless dress and dark blue heels. I wondered if I should have tried to look smarter.

"Thanks. I've bought the wine, so are you happy to pay for the taxi?"

"Yeah, of course," I said, putting my hand in my trouser pocket to make sure the notes were still there.

The taxi left Highgate, got onto the Edgware Road, then went through Marble Arch, Park Lane, Piccadilly, Grosvenor Place, Eaton Square, Sloane Square and finally came to a stop outside a huge red-bricked mansion block just off the King's Road. This was another postcode league entirely.

"That's £32.50, mate," said the cab driver, busily eyeing up Emily as she got out the cab.

"£32.50?"

"That's what it says on the meter, mate. Need a receipt?"

Adam's mansion flat wasn't what I expected. All day, I'd been trying to guess what his taste might be like. The image I had in my mind was sparse. Probably minimalist. Chrome, stainless steel, wooden floors and white walls. Hard. Cold. The kind of flat you imagine a ruthless and successful man to have. But I couldn't have been more wrong. About the flat that is.

"David, this is Adam. Adam, David," said Emily, as the dark-haired, good-looking and well-dressed man bent down to kiss her politely on either cheek. He looked taller than I'd imagined and I disliked him already.

"Hello," he said, without smiling or offering his hand. I figured the feeling was mutual.

Emily took off her high heels as soon as she stepped onto the immaculate cream carpet in the hallway, and then I noticed several other pairs of shoes lined up by the door.

"Shoes off please, if you don't mind," said Adam as he glanced down at my trainers, and as I slid the first one off, revealing the unmistakable toe hole, I felt a stab of humiliation which I tried not to show as we walked down the hallway and into the large sitting room.

At the head of the room was a large white marble fireplace,

with alcove shelving either side, crammed with books and expensive-looking ornaments. In front of the fireplace was a long cream-colored sofa, with lots of plump, richly-stuffed cushions.

At the far end of the room were three French windows, partly framed by huge potted plants, which led out onto a private balcony that overlooked the King's Road below and in front of the windows, a large dining table with a group of smartly dressed people sat round it, talking loudly to each other. The whole place said class, education, money and confidence. In that order.

"Vega Sauco Seleccion. Good choice," I heard Adam say to Emily as she handed him the bottle and an overly-loud voice bellowed, "No, you're joking, really?" followed by several people laughing loudly.

"Hi everyone, this is David. David, this is everyone," called out Emily, with a voice that sounded a bit forced in its brightness. For a moment, the conversation stopped and a few heads turned round and a couple of people smiled and said, "Hi," but then everyone went back to talking again.

Adam's seat was at the head of the table. He pulled out the empty chair on his right-hand side for Emily and she sat down. Then he walked to the other side of the table and pulled out a chair for me further down. I didn't realize we'd be seated apart.

"So, Daniel, what do you do?" asked a woman sat opposite, wearing a white halter-neck dress with a big red necklace as I sat down and looked around.

"My name's David."

"Emily tells me you're involved in landscape gardening of some kind? Are you an architect?" said someone.

"Er, no, I—"

"Don't talk to me about architects," butted in the grey-haired man sat on my right. "Cost a bloody fortune and never finish anything on time."

A blond woman sat next to him rolled her eyes. "You can't

say that, Ollie. Just because the basement extension took longer than expected. It did give us an extra 500 square feet, but you know what it's like, you start these things and then all sorts of problems come out of the woodwork."

Someone leaned across and poured red wine into the large empty bulb glass in front of me, a quietly spoken, dark-haired woman dressed in a black dress and white apron. I turned to say thanks, but she'd already headed off towards the kitchen and I heard someone say that Adam had hired her as a waitress for the evening.

"I'm in futures myself, JP Morgan. Worked in Frankfurt until late last year but Veronica wanted to return home," said the grey-haired man sat next to me, talking to me as though I'd understand what being in futures meant.

"I—"

"So have you and Daniel booked your holiday yet?" said the blond woman, glancing in my direction, then looking at Emily. My heart started pounding, wondering what she'd say.

"No," replied Emily, avoiding eye contact with me, "we'll probably do it this weekend."

The dinner consisted of several courses, each one served on heavy, bone china plates and prepared by a chef that Adam had hired for the evening too. By the last course, I knew I'd had too much to drink. I couldn't help it. Each time the waitress noticed my empty glass and offered more wine, I said yes. After the initial round of introductions, she was the only one person who seemed to notice me all evening and that was the problem.

At one point, I'm sure she was silently willing me to say no, she had a kindly expression on her face, and she began to look concerned as she poured out yet another glass for me at my insistence. But I had to get through the evening, and unfortunately, the combination of pressures was a dangerous situation for someone like me, because my thoughts went something like this.

If I feel unconfident in a social situation, I just need to drink a bit more, then I will be able to perform, be confident. Then I won't look stupid in front of anyone important or successful. I just need to drink a little bit more to get to that confident state.

Only an idiot has that kind of logic.

When the last dishes had been cleared from the table, Adam rose to his feet and tapped the side of his glass with a small spoon. The table fell silent as he began his carefully prepared and consummately delivered speech, which as it went on, with a sinking feeling in the pit of my stomach, I realized was the part of the evening that Emily was referring to, when she mentioned the word "charity".

"As you are all aware, I have been fundraising for the National Trust for a number of years," he announced, clearly used to public speaking and enjoying the attention of everyone round the table. "This is a particular passion of mine, supporting the charity in its work with over 500 historic houses and castles. And I have a particular project that I am seeking funds for, which as you know, is why we are here tonight."

Right on cue, the quiet waitress placed a small, glossy brochure in front of each person. The brochure title had 'Aylesbury Manor House' written in elegant scroll lettering, and the rest of the brochure had several high-quality color photos of the exterior and interior of what looked like a posh country house, along with some blurb about the history of the manor and its former owners.

"As you can see, the 18th century garden orangery in the grounds of the manor is in need of repairs. Most urgently, the eaves cornicing needs to be removed and replaced with new cornicing. Even reusing as many of the existing modillion blocks as possible, it is estimated that the costs of replacing the front cornicing will be in excess of £1000. Therefore, I will ask each and every one of you to contribute what you can. Envelopes will be passed around for your contributions. You can each give what you like of course, cash or check, but we are hoping that everyone will donate, let's say, up to £100."

No one else seemed alarmed. They all seemed to know this was coming. Everyone started reaching in their jacket pockets or handbags and pulling out leather-bound checkbooks as the waitress walked around the table, placing a small, cream-colored envelope in the middle of each place setting.

"Remind me who we make the check payable to?" asked the woman next to me, in a casual tone of voice that suggested £100 was a mere trifling, little more than small change.

"The National Trust fund," said Adam, smiling.

After a few minutes, everyone had written their checks and placed them in their envelopes. I felt around in my pocket and pulled out the last £10 note I had and slipped it into mine when no one was looking. I definitely felt sick now.

"Who'd like to volunteer to be the accountant for the evening?" asked Adam, looking round the table, expectantly.

"It's no use asking me," said someone in a loud, braying voice, "I'm hopeless at math."

"And it's no use asking Gerald. JP Morgan posted record losses last month," said someone else and everyone laughed.

"I'll do it," said the stern-looking halter-neck dress woman sat opposite.

The waitress collected up all the envelopes and handed them to her, and to my horror, she started opening them and emptying out the contents onto the table in front of her.

"What the hell were you thinking of?" whispered Emily as we stood by the fireplace twenty minutes later, the tone of her hushed but seething voice making it clear that she thought I was responsible for ruining the whole evening and she thought I should know that. "I mean £10?" she went on. "Do you know how much the meal alone cost, never mind the wine? You are supposed to contribute to the whole thing at a charity dinner, not throw in £10 as though it's a whip-round for a Chinese takeaway."

"I'm sorry, I didn't have any more on me. I wasn't—"

"Which part didn't you get when I said it was a charity dinner? It's an insult to me, you know, when you turn up here with bloody holes in your socks and embarrassing donations."

With that, she walked off. Unsure what else to do, especially because she made no sign she wanted to leave yet, I returned to the table and sat down, alone. Within an hour, my slightly fuzzy self knew that I'd definitely had too much to drink by now. To make things worse, out of the corner of my eye, I could see Emily and Adam sat together on his big cream sofa, far too close to each other. Almost like lovers. Not ex-lovers, but still lovers. I was almost sure of it.

Something didn't seem right, they were too intimate. I knew I had to confront them, try to win her back, but as I went to get up, my uncoordinated drunken hand clumsily knocked my wine glass over and it fell, hitting a side plate as it crash-landed.

The thin large glass bulb smashed, and the red wine splashed over the white tablecloth, bleeding into the cloth like a gushing blood stain. At the same time, the stern-looking woman sat opposite in the white halter-neck dress gasped at the unexpected red slash, which was now vividly marking the front of her dress.

I could hear myself saying sorry to her, but my voice sounded slurred when I spoke. Then I tried to mop up the wine on the tablecloth with my napkin, which seemed to make the ruby red stain look even worse or maybe I was just too clumsy by now. Meanwhile, the blond woman was trying to dab at the stain on the white halter-neck dress as its owner expressed her fury.

"You bloody idiot. What a mess. This is a Miuccia Prada too."

And that was the moment when Adam appeared by my side and suggested in no uncertain terms that I'd "clearly had enough to drink" and that I should "go home and sleep it off" and that "he would make sure that Emily got home safely."

In my drunken recollection of the scene afterwards, I

remembered asking Emily to leave with me. And I remembered the cold look on her face as she stayed by Adam's side and said, "For God's sake, just go home and get some sleep. I'll call you tomorrow."

After that memory, things were a little hazier. I remembered having to wait over an hour to catch the night bus back to Highgate, sat at a freezing cold bus stop somewhere on the King's Road and feeling gutted, humiliated, and angry at myself for messing up, all at the same time. And hating Adam most of all.

Looking up at the lights blazing out of the windows of his mansion flat as I waited at the bus stop, feeling slightly drunk and slightly sick, I hated every single one of them, with their overloud voices, still up there, enjoying that bloody stupid dinner party.

The next morning, I woke up lying face down on my bed, still fully clothed, my head throbbing. Within the first few seconds of being awake, the terrible memories of last night's dinner party came flooding back, and I turned over and threw up.

Emily didn't text or answer her phone, even though I called twice and texted her several times throughout the day, saying how sorry I was and how I wanted to make it up to her. As the day went on and still no response, I had to look the fact squarely in the face.

She probably stayed over at his place last night.

As evening came and still no word, Emily's behavior, her callousness, seemed more magnified. Just because I didn't have Adam's status or money to fall back on, that didn't mean I should have to fight for self-respect whenever I was with her, I told myself. Why, then, did I want her to return my calls and why did I keep checking my mobile for any new text messages?

Feeling numb, I decided to concentrate on getting the log cabin job sorted as a way of distracting myself. That would help to turn things around, I was sure of it, because I'd be able to use the deposit to pay for the holiday she wanted. Then we'd go away together, sort things out.

I decided something else too. I wasn't going to let myself be put in a position where I had to live beyond my means anymore, buying bottles of expensive wine that I couldn't afford and paying for cab rides halfway across London. That was not going to happen again. From now on, we'd be more honest with each other, or at least I'd be more honest with her. Tell her what I felt, make her see that I was determined to work hard for both of us, develop the more potentially profitable log-cabin side of my business; after all, I'd got my first customer already lined up. If she'd just give me time.

By Monday lunchtime, she still hadn't returned any of my text messages or calls. My heart was thumping painfully in my chest as I put on a clean pair of jeans and my lucky blue jumper and got myself ready to leave for the 3pm meeting with the couple at Corringham Road.

It would take me less than twenty minutes to walk round there, I'd checked the time carefully so that I wouldn't be late, after all, there was a lot riding on this job. I had it all planned out in my head. Once they'd handed me the deposit, I'd head straight round the bank and transfer some of the money across to the property agency account to clear some of my rent arrears. Then I'd order the timber for the log cabin frame and the rest of the deposit money would be used to pay for the holiday. That was my plan.

Just as I was about to leave, my phone rang. I grabbed it, thinking it must be Emily at last.

It wasn't.

I recognized the voice straight away. He didn't stay on the phone long, just long enough to say that he and his wife had changed their minds and they hoped they hadn't put me to any trouble, but they weren't going ahead with the log cabin plan after all.

I wasn't really sure what he said in the conversation after that, something about they'd decided to buy an outdoor water feature for their garden instead. But I couldn't help thinking that maybe it was because they'd caught a whiff of alcohol on my breath every time I went around to discuss the job and had been looking for a way out ever since.

Afterwards, I couldn't quite remember how the conversation ended either. I couldn't even remember how long I sat in my armchair, still holding on to the phone, after he'd hung up. For some strange reason, I couldn't get up, my head felt like a lead weight and I felt exhausted, which was strange, as all I'd done was take a phone call.

I may have slept for a while, but I wasn't exactly sure.

When I looked up at the window at one point, it was getting dark outside. I was still holding the phone in my hand, so I dialed Emily's number again. Her voicemail message sounded as brittle and well-spoken as ever as she instructed any callers to leave a message. This time I did. My voice sounded a bit shaky when I spoke.

"Hi. It's me. Look. I'm sorry. I'm really sorry about the dinner party. I really am. I don't know what happened—"

A beep cut in. The message recording had finished.

I closed my eyes and tried to make my mind go blank. It wasn't long before my phone beeped, and a text message arrived. It was from her. I read it twice, just to make sure I'd understood.

Admittedly, it was a long text message for Emily as she explained how she'd got back together with Adam, but I got the point within the first sentence. It was over and I felt really bad, like I had a strange and heavy weight inside my chest and an unexpected lump in my throat. I'd lost Emily and I'd lost the best possibility of work I'd had in ages. I'd messed up both things through no one's fault but my own.

The next few days, I clung on to the hope that she might still call me, that she'd realize she'd made a mistake getting back with

Adam and that she wanted to be with me after all.

In one crazy moment, I even hoped that the log cabin couple from Corringham Road might call back too, saying they wanted to go ahead with the project after all. But no calls came and as the days went by, the awful truth began to sink in.

Things were never going to go my way and the medium was about as wrong as she could be about my life changing.

Nothing was going to change for the better.

Ever.

Chapter 6

Shipwrecked

The television was still on. It had been on for hours, days, sometimes it felt like forever. As the weeks went by without any contact from Emily, I felt an unspoken pressure from everyone to pull myself together, to pretend to the outside world that my life was still moving forward. Instead, I just sat in my chair and watched hours and hours of mindless daytime programs.

Matt and Jimmy had, to their credit, resisted the urge to say, "We told you so," and their first text messages and voicemails had been encouraging, sympathetic, along the lines of – I didn't realize how lucky I'd been, what an escape I'd had, and I was better off without her. That kind of thing.

Then, because I'd continued to express regret that the relationship had ended, their messages and voicemails had become firmer, telling me I should get a grip, get out and about again, meet them down the bar at the very least.

The doorbell had rung on several occasions and unsure whether it was Matt and Jimmy, or someone from the property agency, I'd stayed low and not answered.

What Matt and Jimmy didn't realize was that breaking up with Emily and losing the log cabin job had triggered something else, a deeper, heavier feeling, eating away at me inside.

The rent arrears. My finances. The whole mess that was my current life, none of it solvable, at least not in any way I could see in the near future, and everything seemed to be coming to a head. I was going to lose the flat soon. I'd not heard anything from the property agency since the last letter, but I knew they'd have some kind of process in action. They wouldn't let things slip. Not a big company like that.

The thought of eviction, the dream of my shiny new life in

London lost, the look of disappointment on the faces of my family and friends when I had to admit I'd failed. The idea of it gripped my stomach in shame.

I got up, went to the kitchen to fetch a bottle of beer then sat back down in the living room and found myself staring at the television again as the next program started, a documentary about astronauts who had had spiritual experiences when in outer space. As it began, the text message alert started beeping on my phone which was lying on the floor beside my chair. I ignored it and took a swig of beer as the documentary narrator began talking.

"We humans have always been searching for meaning and purpose in our lives, to understand our place in this world we call home. With the advent of space travel, this search for meaning has gone far beyond the confines of our planet and out into the cosmos. In tonight's show, we investigate the astronauts who have reported peak spiritual experiences when travelling into space and ask the question, how did this change their lives?"

I took another swig of beer, pointed the remote control at the television screen and turned the sound up.

"One such astronaut was Space Shuttle Astronaut Story Musgrave," continued the documentary narrator. "He claims to have heard profoundly beautiful music during a spacewalk, which to this day, no one has been able to explain. Then there was Astronaut Ed Mitchell, 6th man to walk on the lunar surface. He reported experiencing an epiphany, a moment of profound spiritual realization during his Apollo 14 mission, when he became aware of a great intelligence in the Universe. He described it as becoming aware of an overwhelming sense of oneness and connectedness, a kind of 'interconnected euphoria'. He claims this experience changed his life. After returning to earth, he quit the NASA space program and founded the Noetic Research Institute in an attempt to try to understand what he felt.

"Apollo 15 astronaut Jim Irwin, the 8th man to walk on the moon, claims to have felt a powerful presence on the moon's surface and to have heard a voice whispering to him as he stood looking at an ancient crystalline rock, perched on the edge of a crater at the foot of the lunar Apennine mountain range. Like Ed Mitchell, this experience deeply affected him and he too left NASA after returning to earth and went on to form his own spiritual ministry.

"After his Apollo 17 Lunar mission, astronaut Eugene Cernan revealed to a journalist that he now believed that the Universe was too beautiful to have happened by accident, there had to be a higher purpose or intelligent design behind it.

"Each one of these men believes that they experienced something intensely profound in one form or another in their journey to outer space. And for some, this experience has permanently changed the course of their lives. The question is, what did each one of them experience and what is it about that experience that changed them so profoundly afterwards?"

The text message alert sounded again. This time I glanced down at the phone. It was another text from Jimmy. I turned the television sound down and picked it up.

You coming out for a drink tonight or do we have to come get you!!?

Above the noise and din of the bar, a man called Gordon Hendricks was performing as Elvis Presley on the program *Stars in Their Eyes*, which was blasting out of the new wall-mounted, large screen television. Steve, the bar manager, said that the future lay in providing multimedia entertainment for customers, and unfortunately, reruns of *Stars in Their Eyes* was now his favorite television program. Matt and Jimmy thought it was funny, but to be honest, I couldn't stand the noise, especially lately. Any noise was hard to cope with lately.

"So how are you doing?" said Jimmy, peering at me with a concerned expression on his face. "Do you wanna to talk about it?"

"No thanks, honestly. I'm okay," I lied.

"You still cut up about Lady M?"

"No, not so much now."

That part was the truth. Slowly, I was beginning to distance myself from the breakup. At least that part was beginning to feel less painful.

"Well you don't look so good," he persisted.

"I'm fine. Really. Anyway, it's my round, same again?" I offered, even though all the money I had left was what I could draw out on my overdraft. I didn't even ask for a balance when I withdrew £10 from the cashpoint on the way to the bar, it was too depressing to look.

As I stood at the bar waiting to get served, I heard someone say that they were sure Gordon Hendricks was the second Elvis impersonator to win Stars in Their Eyes. Steve the bar manager said he didn't want to discuss it as there might be a question on it in the competition quiz he'd organized. Unfortunately, Steve had started running quizzes as well as he reckoned it might be good for business.

I was only half-listening to their conversation because right at that moment I wasn't interested in Elvis Presley impersonators or quiz questions. I was far more interested in watching the new girl that had just started working behind the bar.

Matt said she'd started a week ago, when Steve's other barmaid, Frida, had quit. Frida had worked for Steve for a couple of years, but apparently, she couldn't stand the noise of the new wall-mounted television and went to work at the bar down the road instead.

The new girl had long chestnut brown hair and warm, brown eyes with dark eyelashes. Really pretty eyes. She had her own style too, pairing lace-up Doc Marten boots with a short polka-dot skirt and T-shirt and old jean jacket, one hand flicking back her hair, the other resting on her hip. Her T-shirt said Powell's of Portland and there was a logo of a book underneath the writing.

"Who's next?" she called out confidently, looking round at each of the customers all lined up waiting at the bar.

Somewhat awkwardly, I raised my hand and caught her eye, and as soon as I did, I felt really self-conscious. I hadn't bothered changing clothes to come out, and the jeans and T-shirt I was wearing were creased from two days' continual wear. I quickly ran my fingers through my hair as she walked over and cursed myself for not washing it earlier.

"Three beers, please," I said, clearing my throat.

She placed three bottles of beer on the bar.

I handed her my £10 note, she smiled, put it in the till drawer, counted out the change in my hand then started serving the next customer. I wanted to say something else, but I couldn't bring myself to say anything. My brain and mouth seemed to stop working in any coordinated way together as Gordon Hendricks belted out the final chorus of Suspicious Minds.

For the next hour, I sat with Matt and Jimmy at the usual corner table. From my seat, I could see her working behind the bar. Even though customers were trying to get her attention to get served, she took her time and did things at her own pace, which I thought was pretty cool.

At one point, she seemed to glance over at our table and we briefly made eye contact. I immediately looked away, embarrassed. My confidence was at rock bottom. But just then someone laughed loudly near the bar and I looked up again and caught her still looking in my direction. I wasn't sure she was looking at me, but I tried to smile, just in case. It was a terrible smile, really awkward. I felt like such an idiot. She looked away and seemed to laugh to herself, but then she glanced back and smiled too.

Just before 9.30pm she disappeared, and I guessed her shift

must have finished and she'd left for the evening. It was hard to hide the disappointment I felt, but the last thing I wanted was for Matt or Jimmy to know I was watching her; they'd never let me hear the end of it.

A few minutes later, the wall-mounted television was suddenly switched off, and for a moment, the bar sounded strangely quiet. Then, everyone shuffled their chairs together to form little groups at each table, and Steve went around, handing out sheets of paper and people started talking loudly. I'd completely forgotten the fact that it was quiz night.

"So, are we playing or what?" Matt looked at Jimmy and me expectantly, then looked at the blank score sheet on the table.

I was just about to say that quizzes weren't my sort of thing and leave them to it when the girl from behind the bar walked up to our table. She was carrying a drink in one hand and her coat and bag in the other.

"You boys want an extra team member?" she said, smiling.

Jimmy smiled, stood up and gave her a hug, then pulled up an empty chair for her. The chair was right beside me, and I couldn't help it, when she sat down, my heart started racing. I had no idea why, it just did. Then he introduced her.

"Guys, this is Anna."

She smiled at me, then Matt, then started talking to Jimmy. They obviously knew each other already. They talked about a mutual friend who'd just split up from his girlfriend and Jimmy said he was doing okay. She seemed relieved at that. Then typical of Matt, even though he'd only just met her, he started asking her lots of questions. Like what she thought of the pub.

"Okay, but the television is too loud sometimes."

And what she'd been doing before this job.

"Oh, this and that."

She obviously wasn't giving much away.

I still hadn't said a word up to this point, but Matt and Jimmy were used to me being quiet. Just then, a distorted loud voice cut across all the conversation in the pub.

"Okay, Ladies and Gentlemen. If everyone's ready, we'll begin," said Steve the bar manager, speaking too closely into the cheap microphone he held in one hand and holding a bunch of small question cards in the other.

"I'll ask a question," he continued, "then you have three minutes to mark your answer on the score card."

"Are we playing then?" said Matt, looking around the table and shrugging his shoulders.

Jimmy looked at me and Anna with a 'why not' expression on his face, which Matt took as a 'yes' and he picked up the score sheet and pen, ready to start noting the answers. He knew better than to let me do anything that involved spelling or writing. Meanwhile, Anna seemed like she was waiting. Sipping her drink. Waiting. Finally, I thought of something to say.

"I—" but before I could finish, Steve's voice boomed out of the tinny sound system speaker again.

"Okay, first question of the evening. Everyone ready? How many Elvis impersonators have won Stars in Their Eyes? Is it a) one, b) two, c) three, or d) none?"

Matt and Jimmy looked at each other with a blank expression.

"Two. It's two," I said, confidently. I felt good that I knew the answer to a question, especially in front of Anna.

"Are you sure?" Jimmy asked. Matt looked mildly impressed.

"I'm sure."

Matt ticked 'b' on the answer sheet and Anna leaned towards me and said quietly, "So are you a big fan of Stars in Their Eyes?"

She was smiling, so I smiled too, but then I worried that it did make me come across as a Stars in Their Eyes fan, and I was just about to explain to her that I'd never seen the program when Steve shouted out again.

"Next question. Everyone ready? In ancient Greece, what did Aesop do? Was he a) a fisherman, b) a soldier, c) a storyteller, or d) a carpenter?"

"Blimey, these are hard," said Matt, shaking his head.

"It's 'c', a storyteller," Anna said confidently, sipping her drink.

Forty-five minutes later, it was all over. The only thing we got right was the question Anna answered. Matt said I was the only person he'd ever met who knew less than he did. But how was I to know that three people had impersonated Elvis because I'd never seen the program, and I only heard someone say it at the bar. When I explained that to the three of them, he admitted I had a point. And I was secretly glad that I'd made it clear I wasn't a Stars in Their Eyes fan in front of Anna. I didn't want her to think that.

We still had twenty minutes before Steve was due to call last orders, so Jimmy collected up the empty glasses off the table and suggested a quick game of darts to Matt. I was sure I saw him wink at me for some reason when he said it and they both got up and walked over to the bar, but Anna stayed sat at the table, still sipping her drink.

As soon as we were alone, I had to think of something to ask her, but I had no idea what to talk about because I didn't know what she was interested in or what she liked. Then I looked at her T-shirt.

"Is that a band then?" I said, looking at the logo.

"No," she laughed. "It's a book store in Portland."

"Portland?"

"Portland, Oregon. America."

"Oh. Have you been there?"

"Yes. Couple of years ago. Powell's is amazing. They call it the city of books. The biggest independent bookshop in the world."

"I guess you read a lot then?"

"Some. What about you?"

"No. Not much."

She looked at me curiously, so I figured I had to explain more, say why.

"I find it difficult to concentrate when I'm reading. Can't make sense of the letters on the page. I've always been like that. I'm dyslexic."

"Ah. I see."

The conversation fell silent. Most people might have felt a bit embarrassed, being sat next to someone they hardly knew, not saying a word, but she looked quite relaxed, which made me feel relaxed. Then I thought of another question to ask.

"So, who was Aesop exactly?"

"A storyteller in ancient Greece. The book *Aesop's Fables* is a collection of his short stories. Have you heard of it?"

I shook my head. I thought it best to be honest.

"His stories teach a moral or lesson," she replied. "Like the one about the shipwrecked man. You must have heard of that one?"

I hadn't, but I must have looked curious, because she told me the story. Or maybe she thought of the story when she looked at me. I wasn't sure which.

"It's the one about the man who was shipwrecked and found himself marooned at sea. When he called out to Athena for help, she told him to try swimming as well."

She paused at this point, looking directly at me. I got the impression she was waiting for a response, but the penny still hadn't dropped, and I had to admit as much.

"I don't get it?"

"Athena, the Goddess of Wisdom," she explained. "Gave him some wise advice."

"I still don't get it."

"The moral of the fable is, you can't just expect help to turn up if you need it. You have to take action as well. In other words, you can ask for help as long as you like but unless you are willing to make the right choices and start swimming towards the shore, the lifeboat can't find you to save you. That's the moral of the story."

"But how do you know what the right choices are?"

"You make choices based on what you believe and what you value most."

She had no idea that what she'd just said had cut through to a place that still felt hypersensitive, a raw, irritated internal wound, and despite opening my mouth to say something neutral or polite in response, a treacherous need to tell the truth made different words come out.

"The only thing my ex-girlfriend valued was money. And I had less of it than her wealthy boss so you can guess which one she chose."

"You are kidding?" she replied a little hesitantly, a look of dawning comprehension on her face.

"Trust me. I was there at the dinner party when it happened."

"That's terrible," she said, looking genuinely concerned, "but there must have been more to it than just money?"

"What do you mean?"

"Deeper reasons?"

"Like what?"

"Older stuff," she replied, "still playing itself out, underneath the money issue."

"I don't understand?"

She sighed deeply, as though pausing to find the words to explain. "Sometimes we go into relationships because we hope the other person will like the bits of us that we don't like about ourselves. And when they don't, that's when the trouble starts. That's when we start to get afraid that they'll abandon us."

"Says who?" I said, curious to find out where she had formed this opinion from. It sounded slightly too rehearsed and I guessed that she'd absorbed this insight from someone else's words.

"My £60 per hour therapist," she said, half-smiling.

"Sounds like your therapist needs therapy. You should ask for your money back."

"I would do, but my therapist abandoned me."

We both laughed and I liked her for laughing at herself.

"Have you ever seen a therapist?" she asked, slightly hesitantly.

"No way," I replied. "If I need advice, I just ask Matt or Jimmy. Besides, I wouldn't want to pay good money just to talk about my feelings, that's a waste, it's like admitting you can't fix your own problems and paying someone else to do it."

"You think it's a waste of time going to a therapist then?" she asked, looking slightly offended now and I wasn't sure whether I imagined a slightly charged atmosphere all of a sudden. It obviously meant a lot to her but then I felt mildly resentful for feeling guilty. After all, I didn't have to like the idea of therapy. But I told myself it wasn't her fault I felt that way, I shouldn't take it out on her, she seemed really nice.

"I didn't mean it to sound like that," I said, a slightly apologetic tone to my voice. "I'm sure it's helpful for some people. It's just not my thing. Sorry."

"Tough guy, eh?"

We both fell silent again, another comfortable silence, and I reflected on how her kindness and her calm manner led me on to tell her things I wouldn't normally tell anyone I'd just met.

"So, what do you do when you are not going to therapy?" I asked, changing the subject.

"I'm doing a degree at King's College."

"In what?"

"English literature."

"You study books?"

"Yes."

"What kind?"

"Everything from Shakespeare to Eliot."

I had no idea who Eliot was, but I didn't let on. "Do you have to read the books all the way through?"

"Yes," she replied. "We have to analyze key passages, then relate them to social or historical contexts. But, enough about me. What do you do for a living?"

"Manual labor mostly. Building site work or hand-made garden structures if I can get the business."

"You mean you're not an international financier?" she said, pretending to look shocked. "I could have sworn..."

"No. Sorry. Just a basic laborer," I said, smiling. It felt so easy to be honest with her. "It was a fallback career after my plan to become an internationally famous pop guitarist didn't work out. I played in a few punk bands when I was younger, released a couple of singles once and got the opening slot on a couple of tours, but we didn't get anywhere. No one bought the records."

"Well at least you tried," she said, smiling back.

We both sat in silence again for a few moments, Anna picking up one of the beer mats and examining it, but the dip in the conversation felt okay, another comfortable silence.

"So... was it recent?" she asked, cautiously. "Your relationship split?"

"Recent enough. What about you? When did you last see someone?"

"A few months ago. A guy from the course. Didn't really work out though."

"Why?"

"He wanted to be an international financier."

We both laughed. Then she asked another question, and yet again, I allowed this virtual stranger a glimpse into my own private world.

"Have you got over it yet?"

"Over what?"

"The relationship breakup with your girlfriend? Some people take ages to get over breakups."

"It's good to move on, not dwell on things." When I said that, she tilted her head slightly, like she was seeing something in me, but I wasn't quite sure what. Probably a whole belly full of emotions if I was honest with myself, things I didn't want to bring up or get in touch with, and all of a sudden, I started to feel uncomfortable. The conversation was heading in a dangerous direction. I had to steer it off. Shut the topic down.

"I don't really do emotions. I'm hard, see. From blue collar stock," I added. "We don't talk about our feelings."

"Tough guy, eh? Fixes his own problems." She had a sweet smile and she was smiling now.

I flexed my right arm in response, making a fist and patting my bicep. She laughed.

"My therapist reckons it's the tough guys who end up talking the most. He says once they start talking, they never stop."

"I don't like your therapist already."

We both smiled and inside I started to relax as we talked about what music we liked, our favorite films, where we both grew up, that sort of thing. She seemed curious about everything, but in a nice way, although I had to keep monitoring the conversation, steer it away from talking about my life, back to hers, because her life seemed good. I liked hearing about it. When she talked about her life she lit up and I couldn't help thinking, here is someone who is definitely on the right track. This is a person who knows what they want and where they are headed.

A loud bell rang out as Steve called for last orders, and she looked at her watch and got up to leave.

"Oh, I didn't realize the time. I have to go now otherwise I'll miss the last bus home."

I felt a stab of disappointment and I felt angry at myself for feeling it. I didn't want this, I didn't want to feel anything about anyone. Not for a long time. Not after Emily.

Meanwhile, Anna reached into her bag, found a pen and some paper and scribbled something on the paper. She handed it to me, and after quickly finishing off her drink, said goodbye, then went over to say goodbye to Jimmy. After I'd watched her walk out the door, I looked at what was written on the piece of paper in my hand. It was her name and a mobile phone number.

Jimmy collected up his three darts from the dart board and sat back down at the table. Matt followed, carrying three beer bottles and a big grin on his face.

I took one of the beers, sat back in my chair and thought about what Anna had said, because I figured there was something important in what she said and I needed to think about it carefully, to make sure I really understood.

"You two seemed to be getting on," said Matt, winking. "You pulled then?"

I couldn't figure out how to explain to him that it wasn't really like that. It was far more complicated. She wasn't like anyone I'd ever met before and I really liked talking to her. I liked it a lot. But I didn't want to think of her in that way, not now, certainly not romantically, not after everything that had happened with Emily, so I ignored his comment and carried on drinking my beer.

But on the short walk home from the bar, much as I didn't want it, Anna kept coming into my mind. I kept replaying our conversation over and over again, wondering how she seemed to understand so much.

She seemed like a person who expected to have a good life, to love and be loved back, to have good things happen to her. I wondered if I would ever feel like that, and somewhere deep inside, a voice whispered that she might be the kind of person who could tell me how to start making the right choices. Or at least how to start swimming towards the shore.

Hi, David here, Elvis impersonator expert. Fancy a coffee sometime?

Outside the supermarket, I pressed the text message send button and immediately regretted it. I had no idea if she would agree to meet up. After all, I wasn't exactly the most promising of new friends. I was being stupid to even think she would remember me. But the next minute, the text message alert sounded.

Coffee sounds good. When and where?

Chapter 7

The Winged Messenger of Baker Street

As usual, I'd met up with Anna in Camden Town. Each week, we'd get there early before the crowds of tourists descended, then walk around the street market, stopping at the various stalls and shop windows, before getting a takeaway coffee from one of the cafe stalls that lined the street and sitting by the canal to drink our coffee together.

For the past few weeks since that first night in the bar, I'd drawn strength from her. Not just from her clear-headedness and intelligence, but her kindness too. It helped me to maintain a kind of numbness, to hold myself together in the waiting period, the ticking time bomb of stillness before the inevitable storm that seemed to be waiting ahead. At least that's what my future felt like.

It was obvious Matt and Jimmy liked her and I could tell they were hoping we'd get together, pushing me into making a move, but I had to keep clear of any possibility that our friendship would evolve into anything else in case... of what? I wasn't even sure myself. All I knew was that the thought of becoming involved in a relationship made my heart pound so hard it felt as though it would burst out of my chest and then I'd have to have a drink to steady myself again.

This particular morning, after saying goodbye to Anna and walking back to Highgate, the morning sunlight made the housing estate look a little less grim as I headed up the gravel path towards my block. It was amazing how things looked better when you've had a good time with someone. Skies seem bluer. People seem cheerier. Faces friendlier.

When I arrived back at my flat, it was just after midday and as I turned the key in the front door and pushed it open, a letter, half-pushed through the letterbox, fell to the floor. A thin brown envelope lay on the hallway floor, a bright red sticker plastered over the front alerting the intended recipient that the letter was registered, and that delivery would need to be signed for. Typical of the postman, he'd just shoved it through the letterbox without getting a signature.

I knew what it was, I'd been expecting it, an eviction notice. Although to give them some credit, the property agency had given me 24 hours to pay off the arrears before throwing me out onto the streets. A cold rush came over me as I stared at the letter in my hand.

My last hope was my overdraft. Irrationally, I clung to the hope that there might still be enough overdraft facility available from my bank to negotiate some kind of down payment on the arrears, enough to keep them off my back until things got better.

I shut the flat door and walked up the hill to the corner shop and punched in my PIN code in the outside cashpoint machine and asked for an account balance. The cashpoint machine asked if I wanted the information on a printed slip or the account balance to be displayed on screen. I opted for the screen display.

That was a mistake. For now I saw, laid bare in neon green lettering, the weeks and weeks of spiraling debt I'd so desperately and willfully ignored.

For a few moments, I felt a terrible sense of shame, then it felt like everything was spinning and the cashpoint display felt like it was a long way away.

The machine then offered me further options. I opted to try a withdrawal. The machine display offered £10, £20, £30, £50 or another amount. Refusing to accept the inevitable, I pressed the £20 option. The cashpoint now displayed a message that said, "Insufficient funds, please refer to authorizing bank." I tried £10. There was a pause, then with a slight mechanical whirring sound, the last £10 of my entire available overdraft was dispensed through the slot. That single £10 note was all the money I had left in the world.

I took back my bank card and put the card and £10 note in my wallet, and in that strange moment, an idea came to me and I felt steadier again. I'd ask the bank if they'd extend my overdraft so that I could negotiate a payment towards the rent arrears.

My bank had a large branch in Muswell Hill, which was two miles away. It was a big branch office in a large, plush building. I'd walked past a few times when I worked on a building site in the area. As it was starting to feel cold, I buttoned up my coat and began walking to the bank. I had no choice. I had to get money to pay the landlord by the end of the day. That was what I needed to concentrate on now.

The branch office was just as plush as I'd remembered it. The building facade, a mixture of large windows, classic stone and great marble columns, had clearly been designed to give one single message to anyone who stood at its entrance.

Money is God. And we have the power to align you with this new God by simply conducting financial transactions with you within this new temple of heaven. All you have to do is to be successful and wealthy to be accepted.

They'd nailed it in one. The very things I'd tried so hard to be ever since I moved to London. Funny how things become a lot clearer when your back is against the wall.

The heavy glass door automatically swung open as I approached the entrance. I walked in and looked around. On one level, the building was beautiful. The first thing I noticed was the space. The long walk across the immaculate limestone floor tiles to the long marble countertop which sat on plain wooden panels made me feel like I was approaching a sacred altar. But there was no priest. Only a smartly-dressed cashier sat behind the counter. The counter looked big enough to seat ten cashiers comfortably, but today, there was only one.

The smart cashier looked at me and smiled. But something in her smile wasn't real. I got the impression that she'd learned how to smile, a half-believable smile, even when she didn't mean it. The same kind of smiles I saw on some of my treehouse customers.

I watched her eyes flick up and down as she registered my slightly shabby coat and my worn trainers. There were other telltale signs she would have noticed too, like the way I walked. Signs that I didn't have the kind of successful, confident life I saw all the time around the wealthier end of Highgate village.

But she carried on smiling as I explained how I wanted to extend my overdraft and carefully examined my face, my clothes, my hair, before raising her perfect eyebrows as she typed my account number into her computer.

The tone of her voice made me feel about three feet tall. She told me that I wasn't eligible for an overdraft increase and that, in fact, the bank would like me to make an immediate payment to reduce the current level of overdraft. She then tapped her keyboard and handed me a little slip of paper that slid out of the small desktop printer. As the paper printed out, I wondered if I looked as pathetic as I felt.

It took me a few seconds to make sense of the number at the bottom of the slip, which showed the amount I was overdrawn by.

She then asked if I wanted any more help, and when I said no, she continued to stare at me as I turned around and I could feel her watching me as I walked across the nice limestone atrium to the exit door, which automatically swung open to let me walk down the steps onto the street outside.

I looked at the little slip of paper in my hand again and the truth finally hit home. I was on the brink of real destitution. All I had was that one £10 note to my name.

It was all over. I had no other option but to get out of the flat within the next few hours. God knows what would happen over the next few days, what would unfold in the months to come, because as of midnight tonight, I would be homeless.

There are certain times in life when superficial pop songs can touch on deeper personal truths within. Like when you fall in love, and suddenly, the most banal love song lyrics suddenly make sense. Or when you are sad, or depressed and the power ballad hits home in a way that it never would do ordinarily.

I heard music coming out of the cafe next door and that was the moment when Gerry Rafferty's *Baker Street* reached out and touched me, as he sang about drinking the night away to forget about everything. Exactly what I wanted to do right now. So, so badly.

It was funny to think that part of you still hungered after a life that had repeatedly kicked you in the teeth. And that the people you imagined you'd be like one day ignored you as they pushed past, hurrying to their expensive restaurants and bars. It was like admitting to yourself that your dream of a life in London had finally died, just like Gerry said about realizing you were wrong, when you thought it held everything.

I slumped down on the plastic seat in the bus shelter opposite the cafe, which smelled strongly of urine. How did the next line in the song go, I wondered as I sat there, unable to move? Giving up the booze. That was it. Then something about moving to a quiet town to forget about everything. That sounded like a good idea to me.

Three hours later, I put the two large bags ready by the front door and looked around my Highgate flat one last time. A heavy sense of exhaustion was beginning to kick in as I'd packed everything I really wanted and tidied the rest as neatly as I could.

Once the front door was shut from the outside, I took the key off my key ring and posted it back through the letterbox. Outside the block, I turned right, a bag in each hand, and walked up the estate path, out through the front gates and onto Highgate Hill, away from the life I dreamed of having in my imaginary flat in London, without looking back once.

The bus stop was empty apart from me, with my two bulging

bags and just enough cash left in my pocket to get to King's Cross Station and buy a one-way train ticket to St. Ives. As I waited, I got my mobile phone out of my pocket. It didn't take me long to type out the text message. The recipients would probably guess the reasons why and the shame of that realization made me feel even more exhausted, but there were certain practicalities that had to be faced.

Moving to St. Ives, staying with sister for now. Sorry about not saying goodbye, long story. Hope you visit, it's only an hour on the train. David

I pressed the text send button and a little ding told me that the message had been delivered to Matt, Jimmy and Anna's phones. It was Jimmy who replied first.

Where the hell is St Ives? said Jimmy's text.

Cambridgeshire, I texted back.

Don't think you should go. Come to bar and talk. Maybe we can help?

Thanks for offer. Can't stay. Train goes at 7. Sorry.

Okay, keep in touch, take care of yourself

There was no sign of the bus yet, and the road was empty and quiet as I waited. Then another text message alert sounded. Someone else had replied.

I think it's a really good move. I'll definitely visit you there. Anna x

Chapter 8

The Knight Played Chess with Death

This is it. I'm going to die.

The London-bound train had actually started to move, my coat still trapped in the carriage doors, the digital station clock still counting relentlessly on. I could see Anna staring at me through the glass. She looked horrified. Stunned. Her mouth open, maybe screaming, but I wouldn't know. The roar of the engine drowned everything else out.

15.57:55... 56... 57.

Suddenly this wasn't an impersonal set of train doors anymore; it transformed into a savage, terrifying set of jaws. Fear turns everything personal. And at that precise moment, something really strange happened.

15.58:03... 04... 05.

Maybe it was the cold chill of absolute raw terror that ran through me, but from that moment, my mind seemed to split into two, each part thinking separate thoughts, side by side. That was the best way I could explain it afterwards, although unless you'd been through it yourself, I'm not sure anyone would understand exactly what it felt like.

It was as though part of me was fully present in the moment-by-moment horror of the unfolding events. Being mortally terrified in real time.

But another part of me started experiencing things in a very different way. This part of me began watching the whole thing unfold with a kind of detached calmness. And the strangest thing was, in this detached part of my mind, everything suddenly started happening in slow motion.

The platform CCTV footage showed that just over 13 seconds elapsed between the exact second the train started to move, to when I was pulled right under its speeding wheels. But when I thought about it afterwards, for me, those 13 seconds stretched out like hours and hours, everything unfolding in a slow, dreamlike way.

And from that moment, I felt an unearthly, absolute sense of calmness, as though something very powerful was with me, calming me down in the middle of all this mortal, terrifying hell. And in the strange calmness, with the strange presence alongside me, I started making a plan and telling myself what to do.

15.59:01... 02... 03.

Breathe in – can't breathe – plan – think – the end of the platform is coming – steep slope down to the gravel track edge – then I'll be level with the wheels – sucked under the train – come on – make a plan – prepare for the worst – it's coming, it's coming.

15.59:04... 05... 06.

Then, I had another thought in the slow part of my mind, the calm part. After all, in that part of me, I had all the time in the world for it. I remembered seeing a news story about a child, a baby boy, thrown from the third floor of a burning building. Miraculously, the baby landed safely with no broken bones. The experts said it was because the baby had been completely relaxed when he fell. They said if he had been an adult, it would have been a different story, because adults tense up when they fall, so they get injured when they hit the ground. And then I realized why I had remembered the story and told myself what to do.

Okay – try to relax – when you go under – just go with it – it's your only chance – so – no – matter – what – happens – just – relax.

15.59:07...

Footing – can't – "Aaaaaaaaaahhhhhhhhh."

15.59:08...

That was the moment I fell. Or was pulled. Or dragged. There was an almighty, violent jerk and instantly, my entire world was upside down as my body was sucked into that terrifyingly small gap between the side of the train and the edge of the platform. Even though the slow-motion part of my mind kept focusing on keeping my body relaxed, the real-time part of me was definitely screaming by then.

I didn't actually reach the end of the long platform because, for some reason, I got dragged into the gap a lot sooner. I had no idea why I did, but I did. Maybe I couldn't keep up with the increasing speed of the train.

God knows how I survived that part of the accident, being pulled through that tiny, terrifying gap. No one knows why I wasn't crushed into pieces between the train and the platform at that point. No one could explain it. No one. They said it was a miracle I got through that gap alive.

That was when I entered into the real mouth of hell. I went from bright daylight into complete darkness and horror. Something was still pinning me to the train, but I was now hanging upside down like a powerless rag doll, dangling next to the huge wheels, the terrible bite of their razor-guillotine jaws too close to my face, my hands, my nose, my feet, like my body was in the grasp of a terrifying metal-toothed monster.

I thought it was never going to end, the twisting, deafening noise and the overwhelming stench of oil. A horrible pit of oil and noise and terror. Screeching, screaming terror.

I knew that any moment now, some part of me was bound to get crushed. Or torn off.

And in the midst of all this dark violence, I could see flashes of daylight from up above, in another world where everything was safe, and I knew Anna was up there. Standing above me. A million miles away. And I'd never see her again.

Then I heard a tremendous ripping sound. My coat? Or maybe it was part of my body tearing off. An arm. A leg. I had no idea. Another violent jerk and I was spun around again.

Here we go. THIS IS IT. I'M GONNA DIE.

And then I was thrown down. I stopped moving. I hit something hard. Hard and cold. Flat. It was the ground. The track. Yes. I was sure of it. I was on the track beneath the train. The jaws of the monster had let go of me, but it was still screeching over me, inches above my head.

Then I had a funny thought. After all, the slowed down part of me had so much time to think. And I thought about adventure films I'd seen, Bond films, Indiana Jones movies, those type of films. And I thought about what the heroes did when they were trapped underneath moving trains. They always kept their head down. So, I told myself what to do.

Lie still. Don't move a muscle. Keep flat. Keep your head down. Don't breathe. Don't move an inch. Don't dare look. Not yet.

I kept my eyes tightly shut. I knew I could still get crushed by something sticking out under the train and I couldn't stand to see it coming. The noise was terrifying and roaring and never-ending. I hated it and feared it and wished it would end.

Then suddenly, miraculously, the sound above me changed. It was different. No roar. No mechanical screaming. Sounds were still there, but they were quieter.

The train had gone.

That was when I opened my eyes and saw the sky.

A beautiful blue sky.

And I felt the air.

Cold air on my face.

And the warmth of the sunlight.

And I thought to myself, what a beautiful blue sky.

I slowly rolled over and lay on my back, looking up at the sharp blue February sky. It was still clear, cobalt blue, with just a few tiny little fluffy clouds.

What a sky.

The sound of the train grew fainter, but I didn't want to look at it yet, I was too afraid of it returning. Then the clackety-clack sound disappeared off into the distance, and a few moments later, the track stopped its metallic clanging and rumbling vibration and then there was an uncanny, intense silence in the world.

I made it. I'm alive.

Chapter 9

We Are Go for Lift-Off

As I lay on the track on my back, the sky looked amazing. Cobalt blue and not a cloud to be seen, and in that moment, I felt the most intense feeling of being in touch with nature, as though nature herself had reached in to save me. Then I turned my head to see exactly where I was.

I was lying on the railway track next to a huge brick wall, like the walls of a deep pit. It was like being in the mouth of a grave. I realized I was looking up at the last bit of platform, its underside brick wall rising up nearly six feet above me. Then, nature didn't seem quite so friendly after all.

A thought came into my head, this one wasn't good. This one said that no one knew I was here, so another train could come along the track at any moment and crush me. I wasn't safe yet.

Then another thought.

Phone Janet.

My mobile was in the inside left pocket of my jacket. Still laying flat on my back, I fumbled around for it with my right hand and managed to pull it out. Remarkably, the phone seemed undamaged, but it was really strange because I couldn't think straight, I couldn't figure out how to use the phone at all, even though I'd had it for ages.

I couldn't even remember the PIN code to unlock it, even though I'd done it countless times before. Nothing worked. I just couldn't remember. I had no idea what to do.

The phone dropped out of my hand and I heard it land on the gravel of the rail track.

The thought that I'd never get to speak to her again made me feel overwhelmed with sadness.

And then I became aware of something else. Something

important. Something to do with my other arm. The left one. It had started to feel really strange, so I turned my head to look at it. The left side of my sheepskin coat had been completely shredded and the entire left sleeve ripped right off. That must have been the ripping sound I heard. Then I saw my arm.

Woah.

My left forearm had been literally sliced down its length, probably by one of the wheels, ripped open from the top of the elbow right down to my hand, the blood and guts of it laid bare in the bright sunlight. I could see the bones, veins, muscles and tendons, red and fleshy with little pulses of bright red blood oozing out along the butchered length of it. My eyes followed the violent tear down past my wrist to my left hand and then I felt really strange, because it didn't look like my hand any longer. An entire finger was missing, torn right off. I could see a fold of skin and a bleeding, raw stump where it used to be.

That felt really odd. Everything felt odd, and for a few seconds, everything started spinning.

Then things stopped spinning and I felt a sense of wonder again, which was even stranger.

Oh my God. That's me below my skin. That's my arm. All these nerves and muscles and bone have been with me all my life and I've never seen them before.

It was funny what shock could do to the mind.

But this wonderment didn't last long either, because that was when the pain started. I hadn't noticed the pain before. I hadn't even noticed any pain as I tried to use my mobile phone with my right hand. But when I saw my left arm, the sensation that had been drilling away at the back of my mind came through with a vengeance. It was sheer, unrelenting and agonizing pain, and now I was conscious to it, I was in absolute agony and I didn't know how to bear it.

Then, voices. Someone appeared at the edge of the platform up above. A black silhouette against the cobalt blue sky. Then a man's voice called out, "Are you okay?" He sounded really upset.

"Please get me off the track," I begged the stranger. My voice sounded strange. Weak.

"Don't worry, they've stopped the trains. You'll be okay, don't worry, don't worry, someone's coming," said the voice, so far above.

Then, a thud. Someone landed on the gravel nearby. It seemed like a long drop. All of a sudden, a silhouette appeared over me, blocking out the sun. Then another thud and two silhouettes. Then more. I could see their outlines against the sky as they blocked out the sunlight. Urgent voices and big swishy florescent green and yellow jackets and safety helmets.

The paramedics knelt down beside me and started to examine my injuries.

"Please get me off the track, another train—"

"Don't worry, they've been stopped. You're safe. Nothing will come down the line. What's your name?"

"David."

"Okay, David, my name is Mark. I'm going to check you over, assess the extent of your injuries. Can you tell me where it hurts?"

"My arm... really hurts."

"I'm going to give you something for the pain. I'll need to put a small needle into your arm. Small scratch, that's it, stay with me now."

Everything went black for a while, then I came to, aware of them strapping me onto an ambulance stretcher. It felt so good to finally get off the cold, hard railway track. For a few seconds, I felt myself tip up at an angle as people hoisted the stretcher upwards, then with a small jolt, I was lying level again and being wheeled out through the station building and through the exit, towards a waiting ambulance, its blue light already flashing as it waited to speed off into the night.

After a long and bumpy, intense journey that was a nightmarish mixture of pain, disorientation and shock, we came to a halt and the back doors of the ambulance flew open. I guessed we must have arrived at a hospital.

People around me, the ambulance trolley moving again, jolting me awake, rolling down the back ramp of the ambulance, cold air on my face, then bashing through some double doors and rolling along a long corridor and bursting through more double doors into a room with bright fluorescent lights burning overhead, lots of intense voices around me, faces peering down. I was starting to feel very weak.

"Hello, I'm Dr. Roberts, I'm one of the emergency department doctors. You are at Addenbrooke's Hospital. We're just going to examine you to assess the extent of your injuries."

Then a voice to the side of him. "I'm just going to put something in your arm, David. Sharp scratch."

And other voices.

"We're just going to move you onto the bed, don't try to move yourself, we'll do all the movement for you."

Then, words and phrases I didn't understand.

"Okay, everyone, full initial assessment, ABCDE primary survey including GCS, and full motor examination, we need IV access, fluids up, blood cross-match and type, surgical dressing pack for that arm please, quickly as possible."

"ECG machine is here."

"Set of obs now, please."

Someone started cutting my clothes off. I could feel the tug of the scissors.

"The Surgical team are on their way."

"We need to get that arm dressed, quickly as possible. Has anyone bleeped the anesthetist?"

"Where's that warm air-circulating blanket. He's getting cold."

"Check the extent of injuries along the head, chest, legs, look for signs of serious head or spinal cord injury. We'll need an x-ray, Peter, can you get onto the x-ray department."

People were speaking around the trolley bed, all talking a different language of medical science that I couldn't understand, sticking tubes in my veins and bits of plastic round my arm to try to stop the bleeding. Then someone gave me another injection of something, and I heard a female voice explain it was so that they could examine my injuries without causing me more pain. But I didn't hear the end of what she said as her voice drifted off into the distance and I stopped being aware of anything.

I had no idea of how much time had passed, but when I came to, my half-severed arm had been suspended in a hoist sling in a clear surgical dressing bag. They told me it was because I was losing so much blood.

It looked like a joint of raw, bleeding meat wrapped in clear polythene, and when I looked over the side of the bed, I saw a pool of dark red blood on the floor, the blood that had been oozing out of my arm when I first arrived in the emergency department. I couldn't breathe. It was all too much.

"Calm down, you'll be okay. Just calm down and take some deep breaths, that's it, deep breaths," said a calming voice nearby.

I took some deep breaths like the voice said and people kept speaking to me in kind, encouraging tones, explaining things, telling me what they were about to do.

"We are just going to lift your other arm for a moment," or "I am just going to move your head a bit."

Half the time, I couldn't tell who was speaking. People kept appearing and disappearing around the bed. The emergency department felt cold and the fluorescent lights overhead were burning into my eyes and I started to feel sick.

Then a tall man appeared at my bedside. He told me he was Professor Fellows and he was the chief surgeon. He seemed calm, but there was a serious tone to his voice. And he didn't waste any words.

"You've had a serious accident. We are going to have to operate on you tonight as your arm is in a pretty bad way. I need your consent for the operation, is that okay?"

I nodded. Then he walked off and a female doctor appeared at the bedside and asked me if I could manage to sign the consent form. Someone put a pen into my right hand as the doctor explained how badly I was injured.

She told me that the top half of my arm had been sheared off. What was left of the arm length was gaping open wound. On top of that, I had a bad fracture, with the broken pieces of bone exposed to the air. My left elbow was badly dislocated, and my little finger had been ripped off in the accident, with just a flap of skin left in its place.

She said with all these injuries, it was no wonder the pain was so bad, and when she said that, I started to breathe really fast again, and she held my hand and told me to take deep breaths and to try not to think about the pain. So I tried, but it wasn't easy.

A few minutes later, Mum, Dad and Janet appeared at the bedside. Mum took my hand and gently kissed me on the forehead.

"Oh, my love. How are you doing?" Her voice was very soft.

"I'm so sorry, Mum."

"Don't try to speak, just rest," she said, gently stroking my head. "It's not your fault. The police told us, the train driver should have seen you before pulling off like he did."

"Where's Anna. Is she okay?"

"Anna's here with us. So is your dad and Janet."

Dad didn't say much, he just stood behind Mum and looked really shocked, like he wasn't quite there in the room. Janet held my hand, but she kept looking down at her feet and I wondered if she was standing near the pool of blood on the floor. I hoped for her sake that she wasn't.

After a few minutes, a nurse appeared. She spoke directly to Mum, telling her that Professor Fellows wanted to speak to the family, so Mum, Dad and Janet followed her as she walked off. It was only then that I saw Anna. She was stood in the corner of the emergency department, just off to one side, obviously hanging back, not wanting to get in the way.

We looked at each other in sheer disbelief. We'd both been through hell and she was the one person who'd seen it all, close up. She walked up to the bedside without saying a word, her face deathly pale.

For a few moments, it felt like we were the only two people in the whole place, looking into each other's eyes in a kind of stunned silence, and when she spoke, she sounded like she didn't quite believe what she was saying.

"I thought you were dead. I really did. You rolled under the train so gracefully. How did you do that? It was unbelievable."

I had no idea how I'd managed to do it either and I couldn't explain how I'd managed to stay so calm and why time had slowed down so much. I couldn't explain any of it.

"I'm so glad you're okay," was all I could say in return.

Then, because we were both so shocked, we fell silent again, both of us lost for what else to say. And in the middle of all the hectic chaos of the emergency department, Anna took my right hand and held it between her hands and closed her eyes.

And in the stillness of that moment, that was when I thought about asking for help, because it felt like my heart was breaking, because I'd reached the end. Everything had led to this moment, all the mess-ups, the failures, every mistake I'd ever made, it had all led here. There never was any big, positive change coming. The change was for the worse. This road was inevitable. This is where I was always heading. Rock bottom. There was nowhere else to go.

And then, at that moment, I remembered some words from somewhere. I had no idea where, but for some reason, they came to mind.

When things seem at their worst, when all the odds are against you, you are faced with a choice. You can either keep struggling or you can let go.

So, I closed my eyes and let go. I guess you could say I surrendered. That was what it felt like in the moment. Total and complete surrender as though I'd let go of the side of the sinking boat and slipped beneath the surface of the waves to let my lungs begin to fill with water. And that was when all the noise of the room died out and the pain disappeared. And there was silence. And stillness. And then I realized I was no longer in the emergency department because I opened my eyes and I found myself in another world entirely.

Chapter 10

The 13th Man to Walk on the Moon

Where am I? I can't tell where I am. I am lying on something, although I can't tell what. But it seems to be solid as it's supporting my weight. But I can't make anything else out just yet. For all I can tell, I seem to be surrounded by nothing but endless darkness, as though I am floating in the blackness of space.

Do I still have a body, or am I just a floating, all-seeing mind? There is no sound except for the sound of my slow breathing. So, I think I must still exist, as I can hear my breath and feel my body lying on something solid underneath.

As my eyes adjust, I can see patches of color weaving and flowing through the darkness, coming in and out of existence. It's the most beautiful sight. As I look closer at the faint colors, it's as though their movement has some kind of meaning or purpose, like fleeting parts of a rainbow held in place by something I can't see.

My senses seem heightened and I can see everything really clearly. The colors around me are more intense and vibrant than colors I have ever experienced before. Everything is sharper. And when I look around, this world of darkness seems very calm and the darkness around me feels warm and soft. I don't know how darkness can feel warm and soft, but it does.

All the noise and tension has gone. Everything bad has gone away. I lie my head back down, close my eyes and exhale, slowly and deeply...

Peace.

I draw in another breath and open my eyes, slowly. Just to make sure. This must be what it's like to die. Oh. Oh. Hang on. Maybe I have just died?

I should be scared out of my wits, finding myself alone in this strange, dark world, floating in endless blackness, not sure whether I've just died or not. But I'm not. Not at all. I'm not scared because as soon as I open my eyes, I am aware of a deep, overwhelming sense that I am being cared for in this new place. I don't know how I know this, I just do. Everything is okay.

As far as I can tell, I am alone here. I half-sense something near, just below the horizon of my conscious awareness, although I can't see what it is yet. But because I feel alone, a question forms in my mind. Not an urgent question, more of a calm, curious one aimed at no one in particular, because there is no one around to ask. But I ask it anyway.

Where am I?

I know that I am lying flat on my back but can't see what I am lying on. So, I turn my head to look over my left shoulder to see what's underneath me. As far as I can tell, I am lying on what looks like a stone slab. Like an old stone altar in an ancient monument. But although the great slab seems to be made of slate, it doesn't feel hard at all. On the contrary, it feels pleasantly warm and comfortable, as though I am lying on the softest and most welcoming of beds. Strange.

I lift my head a little further, so that I can look down at my body. The creased, bloodied hospital gown has gone. Now I am naked, except for a silver blue-colored cloth that covers the lower half of my body, hanging down over the sides of the grey slab in soft fine folds.

The cloth is like nothing I have ever seen before. At first glance, I think it's made of fine satin or silk, it feels so smooth and gentle on my skin and it seems to be reflecting light from somewhere. But then it shimmers like rippling liquid when I move underneath it. I've never seen material do that. Ever.

I wonder why I don't feel cold, the cloth looks so thin and

fragile, but for some reason I don't. For some reason, everything feels just right.

That's when I realize something. All the pain has disappeared from my body. Moments ago, I had been in agony, fighting waves of intense pain. But now all that has gone. How did that happen? Am I really dead?

Like someone who, on some deep level, already accepts the strangeness of his reality, I calmly gaze upwards to see what is overhead in this new world.

Floating above the slab are three large symmetrical, rectangular-shaped grids, side by side in a row, like wide overhead light boxes of some kind. I can't see if they are attached to anything; they seem to be just floating above me, giving out a white light that illuminates my entire body. That's the light I can see reflecting in the shimmering blue cloth.

Although I am curious about my surroundings, it's the white light above my head that now draws my attention. I lie my head back down on the slate slab and look directly into this light. It's different to the harsh synthetic light of the fluorescent strips in the emergency department. There is a warmth to this light that feels pure and natural and doesn't burn my eyes, and I want to stay exactly where I am, lying on my back looking up into this light forever. Because this new world and this light feel so wondrous and fantastic and alive.

In this eternal, timeless moment, something else draws my attention away from the light boxes and I look to the side to see what it is. What I see is a Being, now standing at my feet. I can sense something fantastic and powerful in its presence and I feel the most overwhelming, indescribable love radiating from it.

When I look closer at this Being, I can see that it isn't feminine or masculine. It's neither, yet it's both at the same time. A strange and beautiful Being with white blond, wavy hair and pale, luminous skin and a simple black cloth worn over its body. And I feel safe, because I feel total trust in the love and compassion of this Being. There is no feeling of fear, no questioning, only acceptance. I feel loved to the very core of my soul.

And now there are two more Beings, one stood on either side of me. I feel no fear of them at all. Somehow, I know that they are a natural part of this new reality. They look human, feminine and both have warm darker skin tones and jet-black hair, which makes me think they look Brazilian or Native American. But one thing is for certain. I know they are not from the world I've left behind.

The two Beings move their outstretched hands over different areas of my body, very slowly and very gently, as though healing me with some kind of energy that I can't see. As they move, they don't say a word and neither do I. Even though I wonder and marvel at their presence, there is no need to speak of it because when I look in their eyes, I feel the most beautiful expression of warmth and love. But not through words. The Beings around me communicate this love and reassurance telepathically. They seem to know what I am thinking, and I can feel what they are thinking as well.

Relax, you are safe, everything is well. You are loved.

I raise my head again to look at my injured arm and it is completely healed. The horrible, gaping, violent wound has gone.

Then I have another thought. Maybe I am being prepared for something, although I don't worry what it is. I have nothing to worry about in this place. I am happy to stay in this eternal place forever.

From that small thought, a bigger thought emerges. Am I ever going to be returned back to where I've just come from, the world of my accident and the hospital and pain? Or have I really passed on, never to return?

Right now, I don't care if I never go back to that world. I am so peaceful and happy in this place. There is no question about it, I want to stay here forever. Even if it means I am dead.

I close my eyes as they continue to work and become aware of an overwhelming sensation of peace. Not a sleepy peace, but a sensation of an absolute, true and restful peace beyond words.

And then something else draws my attention which is surely new, since I would have noticed it if it was there before. Yet somehow it has been there the whole time, because on some level, I've felt the presence of it ever since I arrived, on the edge of my awareness. Now I see it, and in all my life, I never dreamt I would see such a beautiful sight with my own eyes. A swirling, three-dimensional tunnel of radiant light, with a glowing luminosity and intensity that is blindingly brilliant, and yet I can look straight into it.

The radiance becomes more and more intense as the tunnel of light slowly rotates and colors within the light arc into existence, then disappear, then form like brilliant flames again. The outer half of the tunnel swirls and ebbs, flaming hues of orange and red and gold slowly erupting, flaring and weaving their way towards the edge of the brilliant radiance.

Towards the center, flames of yellow become flames of cream, then transform themselves into white light. And at the very center of this radiant tunnel is the purity of white light itself.

Perfection.

In the presence of this luminous and wondrous Light, I become aware of every single cell of my body as they begin to vibrate with its love. And I feel more alive than I have ever done so before, because this is the Light of all Light. The Light of pure, unconditional Love.

Held in this endless, eternal moment, I realize something. This is it, I have passed over. I have died and they are getting me ready for something. I am being prepared to go on to somewhere else now.

At the realization of this, I feel certain I am dead because this world is not the physical world, and this infinite force of Love is not an earthly love. But I have no fear about having passed over, no reluctance to accept my death or desire to leave this place. I accept it all, wholly and fully and willingly.

All the bad feelings of anxiety and worry have completely gone, along with the pain from the accident. Time is now endless and space, now infinite and boundless, and I have no idea whether I have been here minutes, years or for all of eternity itself.

Then another thought comes into my head. It is as though a long-forgotten, distant memory has floated to the surface.

My family. I wonder if they are okay, now that I'm dead. It's strange, but in this peaceful place, I feel no sense of urgency or distress about their grief, more of a vague, half-remembered curiosity about a group of people whose situation seems far removed from anything that is real and important now.

This vagueness isn't a lack of love for them; it's borne out of the certain realization that the place I am in now is the true reality, whereas my old world is just an illusion. I know that now. And because everyone comes here when they die, there is nothing to really worry about. I will see my family again when they eventually pass over and each one of them will experience the love and beauty I am experiencing here. That makes me feel happy, so the idea of seeing them grieving in my old world doesn't worry me in the slightest.

As I remember my family, I then wonder if I can see them in the old world and another idea forms, too simple at first, the idea that this new world is literally floating above my old world. But somehow, the idea takes hold and I imagine that if I lean right over the edge of the slab, I might be able to look down at the hospital scene below. And if I can lean over far enough, I might see them all stood there, gathered round my dead body lying in the hospital bed.

And like someone who expects to see exactly what he imagines, I lean over and look down over the side of the slab on which I am lying. But what I see is totally unexpected and it is not my old world at all.

It is a cascading waterfall of galaxies before me.

No.

Entire universes.

No. Whole dimensions.

Billions of tiny stars, forever falling from the outer horizon of a huge, circular waterfall, all travelling in the same direction, downwards, ever downwards, into an infinite spiral at its heart.

Billions and billions of stars, so many glittering stars across each universe that I can never hope to take them all in. I feel like I am seeing nothing less than the true nature of reality itself. It is so much more breathtaking and unimaginable than any of the two-dimensional images of the universe I saw in books or films when I was alive.

And now I understand that I am not actually in a small, dark, warmly-lit room at all. I am, in fact, lying amongst the stars.

There are no thoughts now. Only an overwhelming sense of infinite interconnectedness. Finally, after a minute or all of eternity, I am not sure which, I draw my gaze away from the waterfall and lie my head back down onto the slab, grinning in absolute joy and wonderment.

Then thoughts come into my head again because I try to grasp the enormity of it all. And once again, my gaze is drawn back to the great luminous, brilliant tunnel of radiant light, swirling at my feet, because now I understand what I am meant to. I understand where all the Love is coming from, the Love coming through the hands of the Beings, the Love in the colors of the darkness and in the waterfall of galaxies and stars. All this Love is coming from the radiant, incandescent Light itself.

And I laugh. The Renaissance painters got it so wrong when they painted the Creator as a bearded man, poised in the sky. They should have painted the Light instead. The Light is the bringer of everything and the place where all things return. This is the source of all Love, this is Life itself.

This is such a powerful realization. I feel so happy, so peaceful, so glad that I am with the Light. I have come home. I close my eyes in peace and all the galaxies and stars turn inside me, then—

Part II

The Friendly Universe

Chapter 11

The Eagle Has Landed

Okay. Camera rolling... 5, 4, 3, 2, 1.

"Here is the lunchtime BBC News. First, a man has been badly injured after falling under a train at Huntingdon railway station. It was believed he was seeing his girlfriend onto the train when the accident happened. Rail services were suspended while emergency crews worked to rescue him."

Later...

"On tonight's news, we report on a man's horrific accident after becoming trapped in the doors of a moving train. He was seeing off a friend at Huntingdon railway station when he got dragged off the end of the platform and under the train. This afternoon he had a second operation at Addenbrooke's Hospital to save his arm. Before he went into surgery, his family spoke exclusively to ITN's Matthew Hudson, who has this report for us."

"David was seeing a friend off at Huntingdon railway station when his coat became trapped in the train door and he was dragged along the platform and very nearly to his death. He is now in Addenbrooke's Hospital with surgeons battling to save his arm, and the train operators have launched an enquiry to find out what happened. For now, David is in shock and pain, but also aware that he's lucky to be alive. Matthew Hudson, ITN News, Cambridge."

"Ouch."

"Sorry."

"It's okay, honestly. Don't worry about it."

It really did hurt, but I wasn't going to say anything. When I came around after the first operation, I tried to think of a reason why my legs were burning so badly. I couldn't remember them burning like that in the emergency department, so I asked the nurse why they were, and she carefully lifted the bed sheet that was draped over my legs and showed me why. My legs were bandaged all the way up to the top. She explained that the plastic surgeons had had to take large skin grafts from both thighs to rebuild my arm. That was when I understood why they hurt so much.

Three days and two operations later, this was the first morning I felt vaguely human again. Apparently, I'd had quite a few visitors already. My family, Anna and, as one older nurse put it, "two very good-looking lads". It had to be Matt and Jimmy. I wasn't strong enough yet to reach over to pick up any of the cards on the bedside table, but I could guess which one was from them, a mile off.

"It was on the news again last night, your accident," Julie the nurse said, watching the blood pressure machine whirr into action as the bladder cuff on my right arm inflated and squeezed tighter and tighter. "They said you're lucky to be alive."

"I guess I am," I replied, trying hard not to wince as she unintentionally sent shooting pains up my arm when she removed the bladder cuff and repositioned the stiff hospital pillow that was supporting my bandaged elbow and shoulder of my left arm.

It didn't look like my arm anymore, it looked like a strange piece of pale, swollen, bloody meat. But Julie said I needed to sit up in bed for breakfast, so she needed to move it.

The telltale sign that breakfast had appeared on the main ward arrived long before the bowl of lukewarm porridge and stewed mug of tea appeared in my side room, as the unmistakable odor of hospital catering hit my nostrils. It was a strange combination of disinfectant and the smell of industrial food preparation, and I knew I'd never forget that slightly metallic smell as long as I lived.

Just after 9.30am, when the breakfast trays had been cleared away, it was as though the seas had parted and all the early morning chaos of the ward had become instantly hushed as Professor Fellows strode into my room followed by a small group of people who filed in behind him, silently arranging themselves in a semicircle as he took up his position of authority at the end of my bed.

Everyone stared at me as Professor Fellows flicked through a bulging manila folder he was carrying, which I guessed contained my hospital notes.

He was just as impressive as I remembered him from the first night in the emergency department. Confident, highly focused, clearly used to making profound decisions, taking charge, saving lives. The people stood around him seemed smaller by comparison and none of them uttered a word, not unless he spoke to them. Julie had already explained to me that they were medical students, and this was how they were taught. It struck me as a strange way to learn.

I watched him closely as he fired questions at Julie about my wound dressings, and all the while, a dozen pairs of silent, curious eyes continued to stare at me. Feeling increasingly self-conscious in the tense atmosphere of the crowded room, I didn't know where to look. In hospital, even if you felt shy, you couldn't be, because there was no privacy anywhere.

As Julie answered his questions, he scribbled on one of the pages in the folder, then closed it and put his pen back in his shirt pocket. He then turned the focus of his impressive, intense gaze in my direction and I felt like I was suddenly in the glare of a powerful spotlight.

"So, David. How are you feeling today?"

"Much better, thank you," I said, an unmistakable tone of gratitude clearly evident in my voice because I was convinced, emphatically, that he had single-handedly saved both my arm and my life in the operating theatre that first night.

"And the pain?" he asked, sounding pleased. "Have we got that under control?"

"I'm still a bit sore. But not as bad as yesterday."

"Good," he replied, smiling. "Let's get you up to sit in the chair tomorrow, see how that goes." Without a word, he handed the manila folder to one of the medical students and turned to walk towards the door. It was now or never. I cleared my throat.

"Er, Professor, before you go, can I ask you something?"

"Of course," he replied, turning back to face me. "Ask away. Whatever you like."

"The thing is, I don't understand why... how... I'm feeling okay without...?"

"Without alcohol?" he said, blandly.

"Yes," I said, feeling a surge of shame rise up inside as I admitted it. Maybe some people found it easy to talk about their drinking addiction in front of a room full of strangers. But not me, not now, in front of all these silent, staring faces. Maybe he saw that, because he chewed his lip for a moment, then walked round the side of the bed and sat down on the orange plastic visitor's chair next to the bedside table.

"You've been getting a drug called Chlordiazepoxide. We've given you this because your body had become used to alcohol, so the drug has helped you to cope with the physical side of your withdrawal symptoms," he explained, his voice softer now, as though we were the only two people in the room. "But we can't just deal with the physical, we have to look at the psychological side of your addiction as well, so I've asked one of my colleagues, Dr. Irene Wallis, to see you over the next few days. She's a psychotherapist and very experienced in this area. I'm confident she'll be able to help. Is that okay?"

I felt a moment of sheer relief deep inside and I could have hugged him there and then if I had full use of both arms. "Yes. Definitely. Thanks."

And with that, he smiled again, gave me a reassuring tap on

the shoulder then got up and left the room, followed by all the silent observers who filed out in a single line after him, some of them glancing back at me and smiling as they went out the door, in what I took to be a silent thumbs up.

The consultant's ward round was obviously the peak of the daily hospital schedule, and apart from the busy nurses who came in to take my pulse and blood pressure every few hours, after that I was left largely alone, propped up in bed by a mound of pillows, waiting for the long hospital day to pass and the evening visiting hours to start.

After dinner, Janet arrived. The sun was setting outside the window when she walked in, and the fading light was nice, even for a magnolia-toned hospital side room.

"You're looking better," she said cheerfully as she sat down in the orange plastic visitor's chair.

"I am better, but I'm worried about you. Are you alright?" I asked, concerned at how pale she looked.

"I'm fine. Honestly. Probably still shocked at everything that's happened. Funny thing is, you're so calm about it all," she said, a look of disbelief on her face. "I mean it's bonkers really, considering everything you've been through. I still can't get over it. We go off for the weekend to give you a bit of space for Anna's visit, the next thing, we get that awful phone call from the police. There was me thinking how nice it would be for you two to get together, and you go and get yourself pulled under a train!" She sighed deeply, shaking her head in disbelief. She was right. She was still in shock.

"Did you get everything?" I asked, trying to steer the subject away from the accident. The carrier bag by the side of her chair was bulging and I was anxious to know if she'd brought in what I'd asked her to.

"Yes, but what's it all for?" she asked, reaching into the bag to pull out a sketchpad, several good quality pencils, an eraser, and a battery-operated pencil sharpener, all of which was then laid out in a neat pile on the small bedside table.

I looked her squarely in the eyes and suddenly my heart started racing as I knew the moment had come. I'd been thinking about this moment a lot, what I'd say and how she might react to it. I cleared my throat, took a deep breath and reached for the first words that came to mind. Best to get it over and done with.

"Listen. I've got something to tell you. Something really important. Then you'll understand why I need this stuff."

It was such a relief to let it all out, how I'd left my body and found myself with the Beings of Light and the slate slab and the waterfall of galaxies, the stars and the shimmering blue cloth and the unconditional Love that came from the Light. I finished by explaining how I'd found myself back in the emergency department afterwards.

"Honestly, I felt like I was being dragged back to this world by an invisible force and I really didn't want to come back. Not one bit. But it happened in an instant, like I'd suddenly crashed through some invisible barrier. Next thing I knew, I was back in the Emergency Department lying back underneath the florescent strip lighting. It was like I'd crash-landed. At first, I couldn't bear the thought of returning, but then I realized something. I was supposed to come back. I was helped in the accident, I was meant to survive so that I could experience that other world and I've been sent back here for a reason. I'm supposed to show people what that world was like. I think I'm supposed to do a painting to show them. That's why I need this stuff."

"A painting?" she repeated slowly.

"Yes."

She stared at me, her mouth slightly open, so I thought I'd better explain some more. It was clearly a lot for her to take in.

"I want everyone to see that there's nothing to fear. This place is waiting for us all and it's beautiful. I need to make visual notes, rough sketches while I'm stuck in hospital so that I don't forget any of it. Then I can start the actual painting when I get out."

I could tell from the shocked expression on her face that she was trying to process it all, her mouth still hanging open as though she'd been stopped in mid-sentence. Finally, she spoke, still more slowly than normal, as though trying to grasp the meaning of what I was telling her.

"Have you told anyone else about this?"

"No, not yet. I'll tell Anna when I speak to her on the phone, and Mum and Dad when they visit tomorrow. But I wanted you to be the first."

We sat in silence for a few moments and I took another deep breath as I prepared for the next bit. *Best get it all out at once*, I told myself.

"There's something else you need to know," I said, finally giving voice to the terrible truth we had both so carefully avoided for so long. "I'm going to stop drinking. I've been referred to a psychotherapist who's going to help me."

As I said this, she sighed as though something old and deep gave way inside her and her shoulders slumped forward in relief.

"Oh, David. I'd almost given up hope of that ever happening."

"I'm so sorry," I said. "I know I've made a mess of things up till now. But after what I've seen, there's no way I'm going to drink anymore. Trust me on this. Please."

Slowly, her glazed and shocked expression softened, and as we talked some more, she seemed happier, more like her old self.

Eventually, a nurse popped her head round the door to announce that visiting time was coming to an end. Janet gathered up her coat and carefully folded the empty carrier bag and put it in her pocket. As she turned to give me one last smile before walking out the door, I caught a glimpse of an expression on her face that I hadn't seen in a long time. If I had to put a name to it, I'd say it was overwhelming relief.

The next day, after breakfast, I told Julie I needed to make a phone call. She helped me to get into a comfortable position to hold the phone, dialed Anna's mobile number for me then left the room so that I could have a bit of privacy. She was good like that.

After a few rings, a voice came on the line.

"David, is that you?" Anna sounded anxious.

"Yeah, it's me. How are you?"

Hearing Anna's voice on the end of the phone made me realize how easy it would be to turn to her, especially now I felt so vulnerable, stuck in hospital with 'life-changing injuries' as the professor described them. So, so easy. But when Mum had told me she'd had to return to London to sit her final exam, for some reason, part of me felt strangely relieved and that relief was still there, even now.

"I'm okay, just worried about you. I'm so sorry I had to leave."

"Hey, it's fine," I said, truthfully. "Mum told me about your exam. How did it go?"

"Okay, I think. I still feel pretty shocked though. Anyway, more importantly, how are you doing?"

"Getting there slowly," I replied. "Hopefully no more operations for a while."

A few moments' silence on the line. Then, she spoke again, her words tumbling out.

"I thought you were going to die. I really did. I don't know what I'd have done if..." Her voice trailed off and I could tell that she was about to say something else. Probably about that night before the accident. I couldn't cope with that. Not now. I had to steer the conversation off, keep the call focused on what I needed to say.

"Anna. Listen. There's something I need to tell you. I wanted to tell you ever since it happened, but I couldn't, not with all the anesthetic they've been piling into me."

I paused and for the second time in my life, I prepared to say something that the person I was talking to would probably never have expected me to say in a million years.

"What?" she said. "You're making me nervous. Tell me."

For some reason I closed my eyes as I told her everything about my experience. It seemed easier to remember all the details that way.

"I knew it! I knew something had happened," she said, when I'd finished. "Your face and your eyes completely changed, you looked so peaceful which was crazy, considering what you'd just been through. But I've got something to tell you too. You'll never guess what happened on the train."

"What?"

"After you were pulled under, I ran through the carriages and found the ticket collector and he pulled the alarm cord, then the train came to a halt about a mile down the track in the middle of nowhere. I was crying my eyes out, convinced you were dead and everyone else sat there in complete silence. Everyone was stunned. Then, and I've no idea what made me do it, I stood up and asked all the other passengers to pray for you. Next thing I know, this woman sat next to me, a random stranger, stood up as well and offered to lead the prayer as I was so upset, and everyone joined in with her. It was unbelievable, a group of strangers on a train, praying together like that. It was so moving, I'll never forget it as long as I live."

An image of the scene played out in my head and a lump formed in my throat at the thought of Anna being so upset, crying. I hated to think of her going through that.

"I don't think I would have had that amazing experience if you weren't there, holding my hand," I said, my voice unexpectedly croaky.

"It's like we were meant to go through it together... like it was destined...maybe we—"

My heart quickened now. This was getting dangerous all of a sudden.

"I have to do the painting first," I cut in, all calmness gone from my voice now as I dived in to close off her sentence before she could finish. "I need to sort myself out before—"

"I feel like I'm getting lower and lower in a long list of priorities," she retorted, the hurt clearly evident in her voice.

"It isn't like that. I just need time..."

"I don't want to wait around forever while you sort out everything in your life that's more important than me."

"I'm not asking you to wait," I said, hating myself as the hurtful words left my mouth. There was silence on the other end of the line, and I felt a strange, dull ache in my chest.

At that moment, Julie the nurse reappeared in the doorway, pushing along a blood pressure machine with her left hand. In her other hand, she was carrying a mug of tea, obviously meant for me.

"Oh, sorry, you still on the phone?" she said, starting to back out of the doorway.

"No, no, it's fine, come in," I said, glad of the interruption. She put the tea down on my bedside table and busied herself untangling the blood pressure cuff lead, obviously aware that I was still on the phone.

"It sounds busy at your end, I'll let you go then," said Anna. I could hear the hurt in her voice.

"Okay. Bye then."

"Bye."

"We'll speak soon, yeah?"

But I knew we wouldn't. And I wondered what I'd do without her.

"Are you okay?" asked Julie as she wrapped the blood pressure cuff around my arm. I must have looked bad, because she stopped what she was doing and sat down on the edge of the bed. Nurses never usually sat on beds and anyone who did in their presence usually got shooed off pretty quickly. But for some reason, she broke the golden rule, sat down and looked at me.

"I'm fine. I'm just tired," I lied, but I don't think she was fooled for one minute.

"Everything okay with your girlfriend?" she asked, tilting her head to one side slightly, studying my face.

"Girlfriend?"

"The pretty girl with the big lace-up boots. I haven't seen her around here the past couple of days."

"She's not my girlfriend."

"Oh. Do you want to talk about it?"

"Not really."

Silently, she reached out and gently placed her hand on my hand for a moment. Then without saying another word, she got up, straightened the corner of the bed where she'd sat down, and ignoring the tears that were threatening to well up in my eyes, kindly busied herself with the blood pressure machine.

Later that afternoon, I was sat up in bed looking out of the window. My side room was on the east side of the hospital overlooking the hospital car park, so I could watch the cars come and go below. My arm was beginning to throb, but I hadn't asked for any pain relief as I didn't want to feel groggy. I needed a clear head for what was about to come.

A large oak tree, standing alone in the far corner of the hospital grounds, looked bare in the harsh winter wind as a familiar grey car weaved its way past all the other cars, until it slowly reversed into one of the few empty spaces still remaining. Then two people got out and headed across the car park towards the hospital entrance. Even from this distance, I could recognize Mum and Dad by the way they walked.

I'd run the conversation through in my head a dozen times already, me telling them both as they sat in the plastic orange visitors' chairs. But no matter how many times I imagined the scene, it always ended with them looking upset, or confused. They were regular church-goers after all, and I had no idea what their religion said about the Afterlife.

Yet surprisingly, the visit went much better than I expected, and even before I'd finished telling them about the tunnel of Light, Mum butted in excitedly.

"I knew it! We both knew it. You went under a train and survived it, against all the odds. No one does that without help. And you seem so positive too, despite everything that's happened, even your dad has noticed. You're shining, whenever we come into the room, you're literally glowing. I said to your dad last night, something must have happened, something he's not telling us."

"All these years I thought there was nothing there. I was so wrong," I replied, feeling relief, joy even, at how Mum was reacting.

"You've had so many people praying for you too, so many people have been in touch, offering their prayers," she said, as she took my hand in hers. Then the events of the past few days were retold in great detail, how the congregation at their local church had been praying for me and how neighbors and friends had rallied round too, supporting them both, offering lifts, help with shopping if they needed it.

Eventually, the afternoon visiting session came to an end and they both left, smiling and happy and promising to return the next day. As the door closed, I lay my head back on the pillow, ignoring the intensifying pain in my arm; instead, strangely happy in the sense of overwhelming relief that it had gone so unexpectedly well. Because for the first time in a long time, I didn't feel like a failure in their eyes. I felt like something else. I wasn't sure what, but whatever it was, it felt good. The respect and belief I saw in Mum's eyes as I told her about my experience felt oddly emotional. It was then I realized, with a strange feeling in the pit of my stomach, how much I'd been yearning for such a moment with her, all these years.

Later that evening, after the lights had been turned out and the ward outside had gone quiet, I knew I'd made a mistake not asking for any pain medication earlier. It was no use trying to stretch out my good arm to reach for the buzzer, which by now had become lost in the folds of the bed sheet, because that would involve shifting my burning legs and my still-heavily bandaged throbbing left arm.

Shutting my eyes in an attempt to block out the pain, I decided the best thing to do was to try to sleep it off. But it was hard, still not being able to roll over in bed to make myself more comfortable.

A few hours later, in the dead of night, the anesthetic effect of exhaustion was no longer working and a loud bang outside the door made me wake up with a start. Even though I knew it was probably one of the nurses tiptoeing around checking on the sleeping patients, something about the bang seemed to rattle me inside. My heart started racing and my breathing got faster. Then the bad images came.

The thundering monster of a train pounding down the track.

The huge menacing wheels, inches away from my face.

Being trapped in the oily stinking pit of hell. Trapped and about to die.

And then I felt like I was reliving the moment when I was dragged underneath the monster and I wanted to climb out of the bed to escape it, only I couldn't move.

At one point, I thought the train was going to come pounding through the walls of the room and cut me in two. It felt so real, it was all I could do to not cry out, so I screwed my eyes shut and tried to make the images go away, until eventually, sheer exhaustion and relentless pain pulled me down into a dark sleep. I never, ever wanted to remember that experience again, ever. And I hoped that would be the only time I ever did.

Chapter 12

Irene

"It's likely you have something known as post-traumatic stress disorder," said Dr. Wallis, or Irene as she told me to call her, "which means you are reliving the terror of your accident over and over again, especially when something triggers the memory of it in your mind. This will be especially difficult for you to deal with, considering you are also dealing with alcohol addiction withdrawal at the same time."

She wasn't at all what I expected for a clinical psychotherapist. Poised and elegant as she sat upright in her chair, pen and notepad placed carefully on her lap, she was quite striking to look at, with short, neatly-styled grey hair, almond-shaped eyes and high cheekbones, even though lines and wrinkles were clearly visible on her face. Like a slightly younger version of Judi Dench, I thought.

Her clothing was smart, dark, businesslike, which seemed at odds with the baggy, primary-colored nylon tunics worn by most of the hospital staff, yet her voice had the unmistakable trace of a regional accent which she explained was "from the North". But the thing I noticed most about her were her piercing, dark and deep eyes, full of a kind of strength it was hard to maintain eye contact with.

"So how long will it take me to get over it?" I asked, a little unnerved by her directness.

"As long as it takes," she replied, matter-of-factly. "There is no instant cure. If you want a quick fix, you can be prescribed drugs, if that's what you want. But if you really want to deal with your issues, you will have to commit to understanding yourself in a deeper, more thoughtful way and that takes time. And courage."

Maybe it was the way she sounded, direct, uncompromising, or the seriousness of her tone, or her impressive credentials and forthright clinical reputation, which Julie had told me about earlier, but as I considered the possibility of how hard this was going to be, the temptation to reach for a quick fix must have shown on my face.

"Of course, these days, most people expect an instant cure," she continued. "They just want to purchase a solution in the same way they shop on Amazon. Personally, I think it suggests a societal drift towards consumerism and superficiality. What do you think?" she asked, the hint of an unspoken challenge in her voice, daring me not to be that kind of shallow person.

"I... er."

"Look," she said, leaning back in her seat, her voice softer now. "I've heard positive things from Professor Fellows. He tells me you're very committed to your recovery, so why don't we give it a try to see how we get on today, then you can make your mind up whether you think I can help you or not."

"Okay. What do I have to do?"

"You could make a start by telling me what happened in your accident," she said, as she opened the notepad on her lap, her pen now hovering over the blank page, ready to take notes.

My memory of the accident was more than adequate to describe every strange, horrific, slow-motion moment of it, and until now, I'd done my best to keep the images out of my head, so my response was, admittedly, a bit wooden, even to my ears.

"We got to the train station, I saw Anna onto the train, my coat got caught in the doors and I got pulled under the wheels when the train took off."

"And?"

"And what?"

"You must remember more than that?"

"Like what?"

"If you look back over the last few days, do you remember

having any vivid memories of the accident?" she asked, pen still poised expectantly over her notepad.

"No... Not really."

"Are you sure? The nurses tell me that you've been having trouble sleeping."

"It's a hospital. It's noisy."

"Then you don't remember calling out in the middle of the night, or asking the nurses for something to stop the nightmares?"

"Nightmares?"

"Yes, apparently you told one of the nurses you were having recurrent nightmares, or flashbacks as you described them, about your accident."

"I don't want to think about the accident."

"But it seems you are, with increasing intensity. When did the flashbacks start?" she persisted. For some reason, my heart started racing.

"When I heard a noise in the night, there was a bang. Someone must have dropped something outside the room."

"And then."

"I felt like I was back in the accident, and ever since then, it comes into my head every time there's a loud noise." As I admitted this, I felt my skin crawl at the thought of another flashback "How do I stop it?"

"We talk. You give it time. And slowly, it gets better. Until eventually, you can remember the accident without feeling like you are going through it each time."

"That's it? Talking?"

"Yes. That's how it gets better for you. We talk about the accident and you begin to connect with what you really feel, then everything gets better. And we talk about your drinking too. I understand you were drinking alcohol every day, prior to your accident?"

"I wasn't drunk when it happened, if that's what you're getting at."

112

"I wasn't. That's not what your blood tests suggested either, when you were brought in. But would you agree that you have a problem with alcohol? Generally?"

"Yes... probably... I guess so." My heart sunk in shame at her words, but she wasn't giving up that easily.

"Alright. Let's be clear about this. Prior to your accident, did you struggle with hangovers regularly?"

I nodded.

"Did you feel moody or depressed when you weren't drinking?"

"I suppose so."

"Did you try to hide the extent of your drinking from other people?"

I nodded again, my gaze sinking even lower.

"Then it's likely you are, what we call, a functioning alcoholic."

Maybe it was the look on my face, but she stopped making notes, put her notepad and pen down on her lap and sat back in her chair, her face softer now.

"I realize this is hard for you, but it's good that you are willing to do something about your alcoholism. The thing is, when most people think of an alcoholic, they think of someone stumbling around, slurring their words or falling over in a drunk heap. But many people with alcohol problems can appear as though everything in their life is going well. A functioning alcoholic can even hold down a job and socialize with other people. The danger is, he can convince himself that he is in control of his drinking, tell himself that he will only drink in the evenings, or at weekends, or when he is out, even though he often breaks his own rules. Any of this sound familiar?"

I nodded again, bleakly exposed.

"In my experience, people with alcohol dependency are often secretly struggling with depression and insecurity, and they use drink to deny the symptoms, because they feel ashamed and don't want to admit that they have a problem. Do you think you are depressed?"

"I was before the accident."

"How about now?"

"No, not now. Things are different now."

"Because you survived?"

"No, not that."

"Then why?"

"It was something that happened after the accident, but I don't want to talk about it."

"Why not?"

"Because you wouldn't believe me if I did."

"Try me."

"Okay. Something happened. Something I can't explain."

"Go on," she said, leaning forward slightly, her pen now hovering over the blank page of her notepad again.

"I went somewhere. I don't mean I physically went... what I mean is... I saw something."

"What did you see?"

"A white Light and millions of stars and..."

"Let me help you here. A tunnel of light?"

"Yeah..."

"And non-physical beings of some kind?"

"Yeah..."

"And you felt an incredible sense of being unconditionally loved?"

"Yeah, but how do you—"

"It's not the first time I've heard something like this from a patient who went through an intense life-threatening event. It sounds like you had a near-death experience. That's what it's called in the literature."

"Whatever it's called, it was real."

"A few of my medical colleagues might disagree with you on that."

"I don't care what they think. I know it happened and I want to paint what I saw, show people what it was like. I think that's why I was sent back, I'm supposed to do a painting."

"I see," she said, picking up her pen and scribbling in her pad, and a wave of anger rose up out of nowhere and my voice sounded a little more aggressive than I'd intended.

"Look. It really happened, so don't make it out to be something I dreamed up. If you do that, I can't trust you and if I can't trust you, then you won't be able to help me stop drinking and sort my life out and I need your help to do that."

She chewed her lip for a moment, then sat back in her chair and exhaled deeply, as though a decision had been made, somewhere inside. I looked at her face, trying to read what she was thinking, because I knew things had changed between us, now that I'd told her. After a few seconds of silence, she spoke again.

"I've worked with a number of people who have survived life-threatening accidents. And in my experience, if they had issues before their accident, survival itself isn't like some kind of magic wand wiping the slate clean. The issues still need to be dealt with. If your near-death experience means that much to you and you think it will help you make real changes to your life, then I'll take it. I'm open for anything you've got, if it helps."

"So what happens now?"

"You deal with the post-traumatic stress, and you deal with the issues that led you to drink so that you can live out a life that is worthy of who you are. Even if you did get to peek behind the curtain as you believe, you've still got a human life in front of you, a life with all its frustrating day-to-day challenges. You still have to deal with the small stuff, but if you can deal with it all, knowing that there is a bigger meaning for you, it will help you to make better choices from now on."

"You make it sound so easy."

"Have you ever talked to someone about your alcohol

dependency before?"

I shook my head.

"Can you take a guess at why you need to drink?"

"I don't know. I guess it stops me from thinking."

"Or feeling?"

I didn't reply, but inwardly, I knew she was right. There were certain things, painful things I didn't want to think about, because if I did, a strange dull ache would rise up inside my chest. But I had to do the painting, so I had to do something that went against almost every instinct I had. Open up about my feelings to a relative stranger. I took a deep breath and asked the question I'd been afraid to ask.

"Do you think I can stop drinking?"

"Yes. If you want to."

"But what if I can't? What if it's too late?"

"It's never too late. But the key to stopping is to understand why you drink in the first place. Let me explain. There's a difference between someone who drinks a couple of beers because they actually enjoy it and someone who never stops drinking because they can't deal with what's buried inside. I think that's one of the reasons you drink; to suppress the negative beliefs you have about yourself. You use alcohol to drive all these negative thoughts deeper into your body, so that you can bury them."

"How do I stop then?"

"You deal with what's buried inside. You accept that the negative beliefs you have are untrue. That's how things get better. If you begin to do that, you won't need alcohol in the same way anymore. It won't be easy for you. The bad thoughts might try to fight back at times, particularly when you feel stressed, but perhaps that's where your near-death experience will help. You say you felt unconditionally loved in that other world. Maybe that will help remind you that you are worthy of love in this one." She smiled as she said this, then closed her notepad, put it back in her briefcase and stood up.

"Thank you, I..."

"You're welcome, but I think we've done enough for now. You look tired, you should get some rest. We'll speak again over the next few days. I'm happy to work at your pace, whatever it is. In the meantime, start thinking about the life you want to live and what you need to do to make it happen. Think about what you want to do in a future without alcohol. Identify something positive that you can make a start on. Like your painting."

Chapter 13

Abraham Lincoln

"Julie…"

"Yes?"

"I'd like to do some drawing."

"That's nice," she said, busy writing something on my observation chart. "Be something to look forward to when you get home."

"No, I mean today. Now. Look, I've got a sketchpad and some pencils. Will you help me set up?"

"Well, I suppose you could use the portable table to work on if you can manage to sit in the bedside chair and I can get your left arm into a comfortable position. That might work?"

"Great, thanks."

After the breakfast stuff was cleared away, Julie arranged the sketchpad on the table so that it lay open at the first blank page and put the pencil on top of the pad and the electric pencil sharpener nearby. I was ready to start.

At first, the lines on the paper were barely visible because I was so weak, but by the end of the morning, I'd managed to do two sketches. One of the slate slab and the other, a rough outline of the Being of Light.

Even though I was still anxious that I might forget some of the detail, it was all there, I could easily recall every part of it as though the whole experience had been burned into my mind. And as I drew the outlines, I found myself reconnecting with the sense of wonder and calmness I'd carried deep inside ever since it happened and marveling at the realization that everything I thought I knew about the world had changed forever.

"What are you drawing then?" asked Julie a little while later, as she moved the sketchpad to put my lunch tray down on the table.

"You," I said smiling. I felt so happy that I'd managed to start drawing that I was even able to ignore the by-now familiar metallic smell of hospital food.

"Better make me look nice otherwise you won't get a cup of tea."

"I don't think my artistic talent stretches that far."

"You're definitely getting better."

"Much better."

"Good, because you've got your first occupational therapy session on Monday morning," she said, throwing me a cautionary grin, "no more lying around sketching after that."

By Sunday, I'd already managed to get myself up without help and limp slowly and carefully out of my room and onto the main ward. It wasn't easy; every single step was painful; my body was so stiff and rigid. Professor Fellows said this was partly due to my injuries and skin grafts, but also because of the shock of the accident itself.

"Science doesn't have all the answers I'm afraid," he'd explained. "We can do our best to repair your body, but at this stage, the longer-term effects of what you went through aren't that clear."

One motivation for making my way into the main ward area was the daily tea trolley round. I'd learned that if I didn't get my own tea it would be stone cold by the time the overworked nurses had time to bring it to me. Either that, or the tea would have stewed for so long in the big aluminum teapot that it took on the color of industrial-strength brown tar and tasted like it too. So, I limped up to the tea trolley, requested a mug of hospital tea from the auxiliary who was dispensing it and decided to sit in one of the vinyl day chairs on the ward to drink it and that was when I met the motorbike kid.

It was tough for him. He was only 22, but he'd just had his leg amputated after coming off his bike at 120mph, being chased by the police the wrong way up the M11 motorway.

"Alright?" he asked, as I carefully lowered myself down into the chair next to his wheelchair.

"Yeah. What about you?"

"Tea tastes like piss and I could murder a fag, but apart from that, suppose I can't complain," he replied, his eyes darting around the room as he clutched his hospital mug in one hand, and with the other, restlessly drummed his fingers on the plastic armrest of his wheelchair, his head slumped down as though to hide something slightly dodgy in his eyes.

"Was it you that had a motorbike accident?" I asked, sipping my tea. I knew it was but thought it polite to ask.

"Yeah," he said, with a rueful look on his face. "You went under a train I heard."

"Yep," I said, raising my bandaged left arm slightly.

"Hear you're starting occupational health on Monday. Waste of time if you ask me. Not much they can do about this," he said, tilting his head towards his missing leg and sighing again.

And that was how we met.

On the Monday morning straight after breakfast, a hospital porter appeared with a wheelchair in the doorway of my side room, and even though I said I'd prefer to try walking by myself, Julie insisted I sit in it and let the porter wheel me there.

"It's further than you think," she said, placing the familiar manila patient folder that contained all my notes on my lap, and she was right. I had no idea how big the hospital building actually was and quickly lost my bearings as I was wheeled out of the ward, along one faceless hospital corridor after another, into a lift to go down two floors, then out again along another endless corridor which looked remarkably like the first two.

Eventually we reached an entranceway with a large sign identifying it as the Treatment Center, Occupational Health Department, and the porter pushed the wheelchair through the set of double doors, and I found myself in a large room filled with gym equipment. A young woman in a white tunic top and dark green trousers was sat waiting at a desk in the back corner so he wheeled me over, took the hospital notes off my lap and dropped them on the desk in front of her, saying, "Give me a buzz when he's done and I'll come back for him," before walking off.

The woman looked at me and smiled.

"Hello, you must be David?"

I smiled and nodded.

"My name is Sarah and I'm your occupational therapist. It's my job to assess the things you can't do now as a result of your injuries, then help you to find new ways to do them. I just want to have a quick look through your notes before we begin," she said, opening the manila folder.

As she flicked through the pages, a voice nearby called out, "Can someone ring a porter, he's ready to go back to the ward."

I glanced over my shoulder and saw the motorbike kid sat waiting in his wheelchair nearby, sniffing loudly and nervously picking at a small hole in his creased T-shirt with one hand and again absent-mindedly drumming his fingers on the plastic armrest of his wheelchair with the other. It was obviously a habit with him.

"I remember seeing your accident on the news. It must have been quite a shock," she said, closing the folder.

"Yeah, it was."

Then she sat back in her chair and studied me carefully.

"So, what specific activities do you think you might struggle with now, because of your injuries?"

"Well, there is one."

"And what's that?"

"Painting."

"You mean like painting and decorating?"

"No. Painting a picture and if my left arm isn't working properly, I won't be able to take the lid off paint pots or hold the paper steady as I'm painting."

"Is this something new?" she said, frowning slightly as she picked up the manila folder again and flicked through some of the pages at the front. "There's no record of you being an artist in your admission notes?"

My near-death experience felt intensely personal and I was still cautious who I told about it, but I studied her face to see if she was just being professionally polite or whether she was genuinely curious, and in that split second, I decided to trust her. I had to, I needed her help.

"Something happened to me after the accident and I need to paint it," I said, looking her straight in the eye.

"I don't understand."

Forcing myself to speak as matter-of-factly as I could, after all, this was a stranger I was telling, I recounted the whole story of how I travelled to that other world and came back again. And as I told her, somewhere in the background, I became aware that the restless tapping of the motorbike kid's fingers on the plastic armrest of his wheelchair had grown quieter, then stopped altogether.

"I was raised to believe in something," she said, leaning back in her chair when I'd finished. "I just never heard it described like this. I never imagined…"

"That's why I need to paint it. I want to show people what it's really like."

"I'd better make sure I find a way to help you then," she said, and I believed her, the tone in her voice sounded genuine. As she scribbled something on one of the pages in the folder, I glanced back around to where the motorbike kid had been sat listening. Someone must have arrived to take him back to the ward as he was no longer there.

For the rest of the first session, as painful as it was, Sarah was true to her word and pushed hard, gently manipulating the fingers on my left hand, then rotating my thumb, arm and shoulder to help me get some movement and rotation back.

"That's enough for today," she said after an hour, helping me back into the wheelchair. I was relieved, the sweat was running down my back at the sheer effort involved. "Professor Fellows is hoping you can be discharged in a couple of weeks, so we need to keep working," she continued as she carefully placed my ever-expanding manila folder back on my lap. "I'll arrange for you to come each day, then when you're discharged, you can continue as an outpatient. How does that sound?"

"Sounds good," I replied, still out of breath. "And thanks for... understanding."

"I'm glad you told me. And I'll do my best to help you get that painting done."

Next day, still sore from my session with Sarah, I hobbled out onto the ward as I heard the familiar clank of the approaching tea trolley. Irene was due at any moment, but I figured I had enough time to get myself a cup of lukewarm tea and drink it before she arrived.

The motorbike kid had already wheeled himself to the tea trolley and had his mug of tea in hand as I slowly lowered myself into the vinyl day chair next to him. To my surprise, he leaned in towards me, then spoke in an uncharacteristically quiet voice, his knee rapidly jerking up and down.

"What you just talked about yesterday with Sarah. You know, that weird shit. The Light. The tunnel. Leaving your body. That stuff."

"Yeah?" I asked cautiously.

He looked around as though to make sure no one could overhear then said, "I had that in my accident as well, after I came off me motorbike."

"You're kidding. Have you told anyone else?"

"No way, man, they'll think I'm bloody mental. Who'd listen to me?"

"I would."

"Nah, don't work like that, mate. No one believes the likes of us."

I had no idea why he said that, what he thought he recognized in me that aligned me with him, because up till that moment, I'd felt steadier in myself than I had done for years. The idea of being someone who always messed up seemed to belong to a different life, a whole other existence before my near-death experience, but his words unsettled me to the very core, and suddenly, a horrible realization reared up inside. I must still seem like a complete failure to other people. After all, he saw me as a failure, someone whose word couldn't be trusted, just as he saw himself.

Hardly aware that I had returned to my side room, I found myself sat on the bed five minutes later, when a knock on the door made me jump and Irene walked in, her smile fading as she looked at the expression on my face.

"What's wrong?" she asked, taking off her jacket and settling herself down in the plastic hospital chair beside my bed. "You don't look very happy."

"I just realized something. That's all."

"And what was that?" she asked, eyebrows slightly raised as she opened her notebook and placed it on her lap.

"No one will believe me."

"About your near-death experience?"

"Yeah. I know it happened. But no one else will believe it did."

"Some people might."

"You didn't."

"I might see the world in a different way to you, but I'm someone who has listened to your account of your near-death experience and accepted it as the truth for you. Isn't that enough?"

"Well if they sent me back for a reason, then they picked the wrong person."

"Why do you think that?"

"Because I don't have anything to show for my life. Most people my age have a career, a mortgage, family, kids, nice furniture. What have I got? Nothing. I live in a spare room at my sister's house and I can't even use my left arm anymore."

"So, you think no one will believe your story because you weren't perfect before it happened and you're not an enlightened master now? That's placing an awful lot of pressure on yourself."

I said nothing, my head still down as I self-consciously avoided her gaze.

"Listen to me," she said, ignoring my refusal to look at her. "I've read a few firsthand accounts of people who say they have been through a near-death experience, and as far as I can tell, none of them are perfect, no matter what they claim, either before or afterwards. And if they say they are completely healed afterwards, then it's highly likely they aren't owning the uncomfortable, painful parts of their lives that still exist. They're using their experience to block it all out."

I sighed deeply as she continued speaking.

"If you experienced unconditional love, which you say you did, then perhaps it's a perfect lesson for you. Maybe you were exactly the right person, because your challenge in life is to bring back some of that unconditional love into your life now and show other people, who are struggling with similar issues, that it is possible to do so."

I still said nothing, the part of me that felt the shame was pressing down more heavily than the other part that was hoping she was right.

She sighed, took off her glasses, folded them up and placed them on top of the notepad on her lap as she started speaking again.

"Okay, let's try this from a different angle. Have you heard of Abraham Lincoln?"

"The American president?"

"Yes, that's the one. The president who abolished slavery and strengthened the union of the United States. In fact, he is widely regarded as one of the greatest presidents of all time."

"So?"

"Do you know that his life read like one long list of failures before he became president at the age of 53? His mother died when he was nine years old and the family lived in poverty in a one-roomed log cabin, so he got very little schooling. He taught himself to read as a teenager, but he lost his first job, so couldn't afford to go to law school as he wanted.

"He failed in two businesses, borrowed money from a friend to keep one of the businesses going, but was declared bankrupt within a year and spent the next 17 years paying off the debt. His first serious girlfriend died unexpectedly, he had a nervous breakdown and took to his bed for six months, and suffered from bouts of chronic depression for the rest of his life. He ran for Congress and the Senate four more times and lost in each case. He applied for a job of land officer in his home state and didn't get that either.

"Finally, in 1860, after campaigning for the Presidency, he was elected President of the United States and despite a history of failures and defeat, or maybe because of it, he became one of the greatest presidents of all time.

"What you have to remember is that people don't remember Lincoln for all his failures. They remember him for being a deeply compassionate and humanitarian man who developed a powerful vision, fueled by an enormous spiritual strength. That vision is what inspired him. In the end, his Presidency was the only job he ever succeeded at. And maybe he only achieved what he did in that job because of the failures and defeats he went through beforehand. Do you get my point?"

"I think so," I replied. But I did. I had to admit, I could see her point.

"Failure isn't what defines us as much as what we do after

we experience it," she continued. "That's what tells us who we are. If we truly understand this, we allow life to start weaving its magic and all sorts of wonderful things can happen."

With that, she stopped talking, and after a few moments of intense silence, I looked up at her and smiled. Something in her words had worked and we both knew it. She closed her notepad and put it back into her briefcase.

"Professor Fellows tells me that you are going to be discharged to stay with your sister in a couple of weeks," she said, getting to her feet. "I'd like to arrange a referral to a community alcohol withdrawal group to give you more long-term support and I'd like to carry on seeing you as an outpatient too, if you'd like to continue with your therapy?"

I nodded, told her I would like to, thanked her and assured her that I did feel better, but as much as I didn't want to admit it to Irene or to anyone, even though I couldn't wait to leave hospital, the thought of being discharged, figuring out how to live my new life and finding a way to paint my near-death experience felt a bit overwhelming. I was starting to understand that I wanted a different kind of life to the one I'd had before, a life that would block out the voice that still occasionally whispered in my ear, the one that said I was a failure, but I had no idea how to find it, yet.

Chapter 14

Becoming

How's the new job going? Haven't heard from you in a while. Hope everything is okay? Be good to catch up? David x

The familiar ding of my mobile phone told me the text message had been sent. Just over an hour later, my incoming message alert sounded.

Hi, sorry, been really busy at work. New job great, everyone friendly. Big news! Met a guy at party last night. Got date with him on Friday! Wish me luck. Anna x

As I read her message my mind spun all over the place and it wasn't easy to put together a reply. My first reaction was to text

I thought we were sorting things out, I'm seeing a therapist, I thought that was what you wanted? x

Then I deleted that one and typed,

I really miss you x

Then I deleted that one and typed,

Great! Hope date goes well. David

Then I pressed 'send', then threw my phone across the room.

Afterwards, I packed the last of the large cardboard boxes that were stacked in the corner of the bedroom, but my lucky blue jumper and pile of T-shirts refused to lie down flat enough for me to close the lid on it. The pain from my left arm was bad and I knew I'd overdone it, but the truth was, I wanted to get as much packing done as I could before Janet got back from shopping.

Everyone seemed afraid that I'd injure myself when I got discharged; they all kept warning me to be patient, take my time. I knew they were right; I was still a physical mess. But I had to feel like I was making progress, like I'd earned the support everyone was giving me. At least that was how it seemed in my head.

The problem was, even after all the occupational therapy sessions, everything was still a struggle. My left arm was still bandaged from my shoulder right down to my fingers, which looked like swollen, pale sausages, poking out of the end of the dressing. And walking was still more like a slow hobble. But at least I was out of hospital; that felt like a major step forward.

I sat down on the edge of the bed and looked over at the Rail Accident Investigation Report, still lying there in the corner of the room where I'd thrown it earlier, along with the phone.

The accident investigation board had concluded that the train driver didn't stop the train exactly where he should have done at the station, which meant he couldn't see the CCTV monitor view of the train carriages. They also found that the angle of the CCTV monitor was too low, so even if he had stopped in the right place, the harsh low sunlight made it impossible to see a clear image of the train anyway. And that was why he couldn't see that I was trapped in the carriage doors.

The report also concluded that the clamping forces of the sliding carriage doors that trapped my coat were so excessive, they squashed the sheepskin material completely flat so that the door alarm wasn't triggered. And even though a number of safety recommendations for future train operations had come out as a result of the investigation, it didn't make for easy reading.

The worst part was seeing the images in the report, taken from the CCTV footage on the day of the accident. Grainy photos of me stood on the platform with Anna. Then stood right next to the train with my arms open wide against the side of the carriage, obviously trying to free myself, aware by now that my jacket was stuck.

Looking at these images made me feel strange and I instinctively rubbed my hand against my temple. Whenever I thought about the train, my head felt like it was full of buzzing insects. Irene said the post-traumatic stress would take a long time to heal, so we still talked about the accident, even though I didn't really want to. I didn't even want to think about it. I had too many other things to cope with, like the conversation with the orthopedic surgeon I had in the outpatient's department yesterday. I could still hear his well-spoken, matter-of-fact voice in my head...

"I'm sorry, the answer to both those questions is no. You won't be able build treehouses or do any manual labor or, indeed, play a guitar ever again."

"But it has only been a couple of months," I said, as I began to realize the truth of what he was saying. "Maybe if I give it more time?"

"You sustained considerable injuries which have caused permanent structural damage to your arm. In my professional opinion, the range of movement you have now is about as good as it's going to get. I think you need to come to terms with that."

The man sat opposite in the small, characterless office in Addenbrooke's outpatient department was one of the two surgeons who had operated on my arm that first evening in hospital and, according to Professor Fellows, one of the best orthopedic surgeons in the country. He may well have been one of the best, but he showed no sign of emotion as he laid out the facts.

Maybe he didn't appreciate the brutal impact of his words.

His job was to deliver the medical information, not to hand-hold his patients and second guess exactly how that information might hit home. But his blunt delivery hit me like a physical punch. Literally. Playing guitar and building treehouses were the only two things I'd ever been good at and now he was telling me I'd never be able to do either again. And I wouldn't be able to do any more manual labor.

He was still talking but I wasn't really paying attention anymore and it took every ounce of strength I had to walk out of his office without getting emotional. That definitely wasn't one of my best days. Not by a long shot.

Just then, a car door slammed shut somewhere outside the house and the memory of yesterday's outpatient visit abruptly faded. That sound meant Janet was back. It was time. As I walked out the bedroom door, I turned to look around the room one last time. So much had happened in this room.

Images and emotions flashed into my mind. How bad I felt, the night I moved here when I lost my flat, when my life in London had come to an end. Then weeks of waiting for Anna to visit, then lying in the darkness, holding her in my arms, in the early hours of the morning before my accident. Getting my sheepskin coat out from the wardrobe just before leaving for the train station...

A lot had happened in this room.

I slowly made my way downstairs, taking one step at a time. That was my default walking speed now. Mooshoo, Janet's Burmese cat, appeared in the kitchen doorway and started rubbing up against my legs, so I bent down to fuss him. I'd miss him, a lot.

"Hi, everything okay?" asked Janet, walking in with a bag of grocery shopping.

"Yeah. I think so."

I could see something was on her mind as she unpacked the shopping, so I sat down at the kitchen table and waited. When she'd finished, she picked up the small expresso coffee pot.

"Coffee before we go?"

I nodded and she filled the pot and put it on the stove, then laid out a handful of biscuits, a lump of cheese, some cream crackers, butter, and a cheese knife on a plate and placed it in front of me.

"I'll miss this, being spoilt," I said, smiling at her. "I could get used to it."

"We're going to miss you too. Especially the boys. They've been fascinated by all the metal plating in your arm. They call you Iron Man now."

"Iron Man's cool, I can live with that."

She paused a moment, picked up a tea towel absent-mindedly, then placed it back down again, saying, "You don't have to move out, you know."

"You've done more than enough for me already," I said. "You and Charlie. I can't thank you both enough, but it's time I gave you your spare bedroom back."

She poured the boiling coffee, passed me a mug and sat down at the table. As I ate the cheese and crackers, she picked up one of the biscuits from the plate and examined it carefully, then looked up at me.

"Do you think you'll be okay with..." her voice trailed off before she finished the sentence, but I had a pretty good guess at what she was struggling to ask about.

"Don't worry. I'm doing fine. Taking one day at a time. By the time I get through the alcoholic rehabilitation program, I'll be unrecognizable."

She looked relieved, as though she felt free of a nagging thought that had been secretly worrying her.

"So, what are you going to do, once you've settled into your new place?"

"Try to paint, I guess."

She leaned back in her chair, and as we sat sipping our coffee in silence, gave me another long look, as though she was trying to see something in my face, more than the commonplace, everydayness of it, as though to crystallize her thoughts. Finally, she broke the silence.

"It's amazing. I feel like I've finally got my brother back. There were times I never thought I'd see him again."

When she said this, I couldn't stop the strange feeling in my throat that made me want to swallow a mouthful of coffee, even though it was still a bit too hot. She obviously noticed.

"I'm not trying to make you feel bad. On the contrary. I don't think you realize how much of an inspiration you are these days. I thought I'd lost you forever. But look at you now. It's remarkable."

"I'm not that much of an inspiration. Irene says I'm still a mess," I said, smiling and feeling a bit embarrassed at her words. But she didn't smile back, her expression remained serious.

"I'll never forget the first night I visited you in the hospital. The ward was so busy, but you were so peaceful and calm. I guess it was because of your near-death experience. To go through something like that, to have that kind of belief now, it must be incredible. I can't imagine what that kind of certainty feels like."

We smiled at each other and then looked up at the kitchen clock.

"We'd better get going," she said, "you've got to pick up the key from the letting agents before 5pm."

We both stood up and hugged each other as best we could, even though I still flinched with the pain if anyone touched my arm. It didn't matter though. I wanted to hug her. What she'd just said meant so much to me, probably more than she would ever know. After clearing up the dishes, we left the house and got into Janet's car to start the journey into my new life.

My new flat was very small and very basic, it had one bedroom, a small living room, tiny bathroom and an even tinier kitchen on the top floor of an old converted riverside warehouse on the outskirts of St. Ives. The rooms had exposed brick walls and old wooden floorboards, and in the living room, big south-facing windows looked out over the nearby River Great Ouse, the same one that flowed near Janet and Charlie's place a couple of miles away.

I had just enough money to clear my overdraft and cover rent and basic living expenses for a while from the accident compensation damages. It wasn't a huge amount by any means, but it was enough to enable me to support myself until I could find a new way of earning a living.

The first evening after I moved in, I sat on the large stone windowsill in the living room and opened the window. Even though I still had to unpack the boxes Janet and Charlie had dropped off for me, I wanted to take in the view.

The trees outside on the riverbank had the look of spring, their branches moving slightly in the warm, early evening breeze. The flowing water of the river meandered its way onwards towards King's Lynn and the sea beyond, and everything felt peaceful and calm. As I lost myself in the view, a thought came into my head and I became aware of a dull ache in my chest as I felt its impact.

Somehow, it all seemed wrong, like a case of bad timing, because for the first time in a long time, I felt clear and on track. I was living life in an entirely different way from before my accident and near-death experience. In that old life, I'd reach for a drink at the first sign of any bad feelings or emotions. Now, I didn't, and Anna and my new sober life should have run into each other, but for some reason they hadn't, and I didn't understand why.

I knew at some point I was going to have to talk to Irene about Anna, and with that uncomfortable thought in mind, I shut the window, then turned on the small portable television I'd inherited from Janet and Charlie's spare bedroom, walked over to the sofa and sat down. The remote control muted the sound as I flicked through channel after channel of sport, news, adverts, old sitcoms and cop dramas until I reached channel 24, where a film had just started.

Even though I'd seen it a couple of times before, I turned up the sound and enjoyed watching it again, losing myself in the story, because this time round, sat in my new flat and my new life, the film made sense in a way it hadn't before.

The plot went something like this. An electrical lineman sees a UFO and then his entire life changes. He becomes imprinted with an image that he doesn't understand, and he gets obsessed by it and starts making a room-sized model of it in his kitchen, which as you could imagine makes his wife so angry, she ends up leaving him. But by then he doesn't care about anything except understanding what the image is about so that he can stop all the confusion in his mind. Eventually, he finally realizes his room-sized model is a replica of Devils Tower, a huge rocky buttress in the state of Wyoming. The image implanted in his mind is an invitation to go there, to meet alien life from another world.

The thing was, in a way, I knew exactly how he felt. I could understand the feeling of being totally obsessed by a vision of something, even though my vision was about an encounter with Beings of light, not alien spaceships.

I googled the film afterwards. It said that the film title was based on a classification of types of encounters with aliens. *Close Encounters of the Third Kind* is when humans actually see aliens. When I read that, I started laughing, but when I thought about it later, it didn't seem so funny.

I knew I should be grateful that I was obsessed with the idea of doing a painting, not about building a life-sized replica of Devils Tower in my kitchen, but the compulsion to do the painting was intense, and the longer I avoided doing it, the stronger the feeling got. It wasn't like there was a voice that said, this is what you must do. It was subtler than that, more like a deep feeling rather than words.

The sketches I'd done in hospital had been the easy bit. But now, the image I had in my head was like a fully-formed painting, wanting to be made real, waiting to be brought into existence. That vision was both compelling and overwhelming at the same time, and that was why I hadn't started the painting. I realized I was too afraid to begin, a familiar voice whispering away inside my head, telling me I wasn't good enough to paint a picture like that. Not someone like me. Sighing deeply, I turned off the television and went to bed.

"Hello," said Irene with a warm smile as she opened the door and invited me inside. I liked her office, with its worn rugs, cozy armchairs and overflowing bookcases. Back issues of scientific journals were stacked in several piles on her desk, and several large, embossed certificates hung in black and gold frames on the far wall.

It wasn't a messy room as such; it had more of an air of someone who was far too busy to worry about filing away the journals and tidying up. I sat in my usual seat, the soft armchair by the window and she sat in her chair, opened her notebook, clicked her pen nib and placed both things on her lap, ready. Then we started to talk.

"So why haven't you started this painting yet?" she asked, as she studied my face carefully, her glasses perched on the end of her nose.

"I don't know."

"I thought you said you had a really strong idea of what you wanted to paint?"

"I do."

"So, what's the problem?"

"What if I'm not up to it?" I said, the truth slipping from my lips before I had a chance to consider it.

"There's a difference between feeling nervous and sabotaging yourself before you've even started."

"That's easy for you to say," I argued. "People who paint pictures like I want to paint, aren't like me. They've had the time and the money to know how to do it properly."

"So basically, you're scared then. Of what, exactly? Educated painters?"

I became aware of a knot of frustration in my stomach and an old feeling of resentment surfaced.

"It's like there's a boundary, between them and me, and I don't know if I can cross it. I mean, how do I put what I experienced into the paint? I'm not trained to know how to do that. I don't know how professional painters manage to put emotion onto a canvas."

"I thought you said you liked drawing when you were at school?"

"Yeah, drawing on the back of my school books, doing the odd sketch here and there for mates. That was hardly painting the Sistine Chapel. That kind of stuff is a closed door for someone like me. Always will be. The only thing I was good for after leaving school was ending up on a course with a bunch of like-minded underachievers, learning the mindless task of how to draw slogans on badges."

"Slogans?" she said, looking slightly puzzled.

"Promotional messages," I explained. "Adverts. At the end of the course I got a job in a run-down badge factory, drawing the badge designs. The badge I remember most was the anti-fox-hunting one. They wanted me to write 'For Fox Sake, Stop Hunting' on the badge design. I thought that was really funny, but being dyslexic, I even managed to spell that wrong, so I got fired in the end. After that, I stuck to playing guitar in punk bands. All I needed for that was three chords and a bad attitude."

We both smiled and she put down her notebook and took off her glasses.

"Would you do something for me?" she said.

"What?"

"Stop feeling afraid to start something, in case you can't finish it. You're just putting yourself under too much pressure. Why not just be curious, experiment, see whether the painting comes together or not, and if it does, that's great. But equally, if it doesn't, that's okay too, because at least you tried. Besides, I'm curious. I'd really like to see it."

Her curiosity gave me the courage to give voice to an idea that had been hanging around in the back of my mind.

"Janet thinks I should go back to the Spiritualist Church where I saw the medium. She said they offer spiritual healing, she reckons it might help me find the confidence to paint."

"Well, it's not something I believe in myself, but if you think it might help, why not give it a go?"

"I knew you'd say that," I sighed. "There must be some doctors and scientists who believe in spiritual things?"

"Personally, I don't think you can juggle a deep faith with science," she replied, "science and faith just don't fit. Science finds answers through reason. You can't just throw something mystical into the pot afterwards and hope the two work together."

"Unless they have an experience like I did. Then they know it's for real," I said, an unmistakable tone of frustration in my voice.

She sighed, then chewed her lip for a moment before answering.

"The point is, even if I can't explain what you say you went through without putting it down to oxygen shortage or some kind of shock to the brain's temporoparietal junction or too much carbon dioxide or some other cascade of neurochemicals, I have to admit, you are changing. Surprisingly well as a matter of fact. It's quite remarkable really. So ultimately, it doesn't matter what I believe, or anyone else for that matter. What's important is the progress you are making. And if you think spiritual healing will help you to start your painting, then try it, see what happens."

Chapter 15

Joy

"Hello. Are you both here for healing?" asked the elderly man sat behind the little desk in the vestibule of the St. Ives Spiritualist Church. He had a kindly voice and smiled warmly at us as we both approached.

"Oh no," said Janet a little too quickly, pointing at me. "I'm okay thank you, it's David that needs the healing."

I sighed deeply as she said this, but the man continued to smile as I took off my coat, left it on the seat beside Janet and followed him through the double doors and into the main hall. The familiar smell of the municipal building and the old wooden paneling brought back memories of the night the medium gave me the warning. For now, in retrospect, I'd had time to think about it and had come to the conclusion that the medium's message was, indeed, a warning about the accident, not an optimistic prediction about meeting Emily, as I'd mistakenly believed at the time.

The hall looked just as I remembered it from that evening, except instead of rows of chairs facing the stage, there were just a handful of plastic chairs placed randomly around the large hall. People were sat on the chairs, quiet and still, as though asleep, as a healer stood over them with their hands outstretched or arms raised, working in total silence.

The man silently pointed to a woman stood next to an empty chair in the far corner, then went back through the double doors leaving me to walk across the room alone. Conscious of the creaking floorboards underfoot, I scanned around to make sure I wasn't disturbing anyone, but the healers continued working, their faces set in expressions of gentle concentration, and thankfully, no one opened their eyes.

As I approached her, I tried hard not to limp because the woman standing beside the empty chair was studying me, with a look that said every aspect of me was being examined, carefully. She looked in her mid-sixties, with short grey hair and was plainly dressed in dark trousers and a roll-neck jumper. When I finally reached her, she gestured for me to sit down, and in a hushed voice, she whispered in my ear.

"Hello, I'm Joy."

"Hello, I'm David," I whispered back.

"Can I put my hands on your shoulders?" she said quietly. I nodded to indicate that was okay, and I felt the light pressure of her hands on either side and her voice in my ear again.

"You are going to receive healing from Spirit, according to your need," she continued. "You don't have to do anything, just relax and whatever you need will be given to you. Do you have any questions before I begin?" Her accent was hard to place, there was a definite Scottish lilt to it, but it had a distinct character all of its own, one I'd never heard before.

"No, I don't think so," I replied.

"Then I'll begin," she said quietly, and I closed my eyes, trying to ignore the uncomfortableness of the municipal plastic chair.

At first, a series of random thoughts and memories passed through my mind. Things I needed to get next time I went shopping. Being out with Janet earlier in the day. Feeling slightly embarrassed, sat in front of a stranger with my eyes closed. At one point, my nose felt itchy, but I didn't scratch it, I didn't want to seem like I wasn't focused on the session. Then, gradually, I felt more relaxed. The random thoughts got less and less, until finally, there were no thoughts, just a deep void of silence.

Then, in the blank nothingness of my mind's eye, I could see the outline of a figure in the distance, radiating in light as it came closer, and as I tried to will it into focus, I started to feel an overwhelming sense of love and I knew it was coming from the shimmering, half-formed figure. It was even closer now. I could make out features... a hand was reaching out towards me...

But then the image began to fade, and even though I tried to hold on to it, the image became fainter and fainter until it slowly dissolved. And in its wake, a long time passed in quiet stillness and peace until eventually I heard Joy's voice whispering in my ear.

"We are coming to the end of the session now. Stretch out your fingers and toes and begin to feel yourself back in the room. That's it. Start stretching. Gently now. And open your eyes when you feel ready."

When I opened my eyes, Joy was stood in front of me, about two feet away. She was smiling and her hands were clasped together in front of her. I tried to stretch my arms out, an instinctive reaction after being so relaxed, but my left arm wouldn't stretch any further than a couple of inches out from my side. I saw her glance at it, so I immediately stopped the stretch, feeling self-conscious at the lack of movement. But she carried on smiling warmly as I rested my left hand on my lap and she made no attempt to move or indicate that the session had come to an end yet. For some reason, the space between us felt unfinished, like something more was being invited in.

"You want to ask me something before you go," she said quietly, but it wasn't a question.

"I do?"

"Yes. I can see it in your eyes."

I wasn't sure I felt comfortable with the way she assumed I had a question but annoyingly, almost against my own will, some words popped into my mind to give voice to a vague worry that had recently started nagging away at me inside.

"Well, there is one thing I've been wondering about..."

"And what's that?" she replied.

"Can mediums predict the future?"

"Now that's an interesting question," she said, raising her eyebrows, "but rather vague. Be more specific."

"Well, I had a bad accident recently. A train accident—"

"You're the one that fell under the train at Huntingdon station, aren't you?"

"Yeah, that was me."

"I thought so."

"The thing is, a few months before, I saw a medium here at the Spiritualist Church. She predicted that a big change was coming, which in retrospect, I think was my accident, but I don't know if it was just a coincidence. Do you believe that some mediums can see into the future?"

"You mean, can they be clairvoyant?"

"If that's what seeing into the future is called?"

"It is and yes, I do," she replied.

"But if she saw into my future, then that suggests that my life must be mapped out, and if that's the case, do you think my accident was down to some kind of karma?"

"Karma for what?"

"Before my accident... I wasn't in a good place, I messed up a lot and I can't help wondering if the medium's message was a warning," I said, suddenly aware of feeling distinctly uncomfortable now.

"Telling you you'd been a naughty boy and if you didn't mend your ways, you'd meet a sticky end?" she said, smiling again.

"Something like that."

"So even though Spirit is unconditionally loving, you believe it has the role of judge, jury and punisher. And because you broke some karmic law by living a bad life, it brought about your accident as punishment and that's what the medium was warning you about?"

"I suppose so," I replied, sighing deeply as the truth of a deep and lingering doubt was finally brought up to the surface. "If not, why I was warned about the accident beforehand?"

"Maybe it wasn't a warning," she said, frowning. "Did the medium say anything else?"

"Yeah, something about me being cared for, more than I could possibly know and it would only be my mind stopping me from experiencing this when the moment came."

"Then perhaps you were being invited," she offered. "Not warned."

"Invited to what?"

"To ask for help."

"I don't understand?"

"You of all people should know what that means," she said, tilting her head towards me as though emphasizing her point.

"What do you mean, me of all people?"

"I sense that you have a very powerful connection with Spirit. Unusually so. Are you aware of that yourself?"

Knowing about my accident was one thing, it had been on the news, so it wasn't a surprise when local people still remembered the story. But I was still careful who I told about my near-death experience, but for some reason it felt right to tell this woman that I'd only just met, so I told her the whole story, and as I recounted it, she listened intently with an expression of awe and wonder on her face. After I'd finished telling her, she paused for a moment, then spoke.

"So, you saw behind the curtain; you experienced pure, unconditional love and you now must surely realize that all Spirit wants for us is our absolute happiness, beyond anything we can imagine."

"I did feel unconditionally loved in that other world, but it's different here. It doesn't work the same."

"This is difficult," she replied, momentarily looking upward. "Even though your heart has experienced unconditional love, in your mind, you have to figure out the justice of what's happened, who's to blame, because the mind is so afraid."

"Of what?"

"That life is essentially not on your side. That nothing is going to go your way."

143

"But I shouldn't feel like that, not after what I experienced in that other world."

"But I'm guessing part of you still does," she replied, "and you don't want to admit that to yourself, because then it would mean, as nice as that unconditional love was in that world, at the bottom line, it isn't powerful enough to conquer all the darkness in this one."

"Well it's hard not to think that when so many bad things are happening everywhere," I admitted.

She fixed her powerful gaze directly on me.

"It's essential to understand that Spirit doesn't show up here except through us. Ultimately, it must come through us to manifest in the world. That's why it's so easy for us to create hell in this life. Terrible things are happening right now, everywhere around us, but hell exists here on Earth only because people are still working out the hell within themselves. That is the free will we have been given. We can allow Spirit to manifest through us or we can block it; we can create heaven or hell within and outside us, that is our choice."

For a few moments, there was silence between us, then another question surfaced in my mind.

"Okay. If we have free will, then how come the medium saw into my future? I could have made the choice not to be at the station that day, so how does it work?"

She sighed, inhaled deeply, then spoke again. "Look at it this way. If we are in complete control, you have to ask yourself the question, why haven't I got exactly the kind of life I want? Why have I suffered?"

"That's what I'm trying to figure out," I said.

"Well you could look at it from a more spiritual perspective," she replied. "You could consider the possibility that the spiritual part of our Being has a plan for our life, giving us experiences that teach us to feel more connected to who we really are, to our divinity. So, from this perspective, you could say that your accident was all part of the plan for this particular life and maybe the medium clairvoyantly perceived some of this plan."

"You mean I was always going to fall under a train?"

"It's possible, but just because the big things might be mapped out, does this mean we have no control over anything in our life? Absolutely not. We have the choice to follow our heart. The heart gives us the capacity to make choices that will ripple into our future. Choices such as, should I eat this food, have this drink? Is this the right person for me to be with, given the life experiences I need to go through? I believe it's our responsibility, our free will, our choice, to create a life that supports us on the journey, giving us experiences that make us feel more and more connected to who we really are."

"I've made some really bad choices," I said, sighing deeply as a handful of uncomfortable memories flashed into my mind.

"Such as?"

"Drinking too much. Going out with the wrong person for the wrong reasons and not going out with the right one either."

"How do you know whether they were wrong or right?" she asked. "Maybe they were exactly what you needed to experience at that particular time, to gain a deeper understanding of yourself, and maybe you were exactly what they needed too."

"So, if everything is mapped out," I asked, trying to fit all the pieces of her answers together in my head, "does that include all the bad things?"

"It's possible we decide, before we come here, to take on a difficult task such as an illness or an addiction, in order to learn something," she replied, looking thoughtful as though she was choosing her words carefully. "And if you believe that, then maybe the life you have lived so far is exactly the life you were meant to live and you have been given exactly what you needed, to find your way back to Spirit. Perhaps you were so full of self-doubt, that Spirit had to find a way of letting you experience, firsthand, what unconditional love felt like, so that you could learn to accept and hold yourself in a more loving way in the future. Maybe that's why you had your near-death experience."

She fell silent and we stared at each other, and still the space between us felt unfinished, like something more was to be said. I tried to ignore the sound of plastic chairs being stacked behind me and the sudden brightness of overhead lighting as the main hall lights were switched on, signaling that the weekly healing session had come to an end, because I had one more question I wanted to ask.

"What did you mean exactly when you said the medium's message was an invitation?"

She looked upwards momentarily, then back at me again. "Maybe she was reminding you to ask for help to find the self-love and compassion you deserve, for the suffering you were about to endure. And to remember that we live in a Universe that offers redemption. Perhaps that was the purpose of the message."

She seemed momentarily awed as she spoke, as though she was lost in the wonder of what she was saying, and as I sat there, in the hard, plastic chair in the brightly-lit municipal hall, something inside me, something visceral, gave way, as though a long-held doubt had been released and, in doing so, had dissolved into the light of day.

"Thank you so much," I said. "What you've said has really helped."

"I'm glad," she replied, beaming.

"Can I come again next week?" I asked, reluctantly getting up from the chair, stiff from sitting in one position for so long.

She nodded. "Of course you can. And remember. If you know how to listen, you will be guided as to the next step. Just be open to it and things will become clearer."

As I walked across the main hall towards the exit doors, where Janet was still sat waiting, I knew exactly what she meant, because some sleeping part of me felt like it had been brought to life in that conversation, still tentative, not yet fully developed, but it was now there, at the surface, floating up at last, no longer weighed down by the gloomy concerns of karma. I could even name it. It was the confidence, the self-belief to start the painting.

"You were in there a long time. What was it like?" asked Janet, looking at me with a curious expression on her face.

"It was great. And now I need a studio," I said, surprised at the newfound certainty in my voice, "to start the painting."

The funny thing about life, or fate, or whatever you want to call it, is that once you've made your mind up about something, really made up your mind, then life has a way of putting what you needed in your path. As least that's what it felt like.

So, when Janet and I left the church and started walking back to the car park and we bumped into two of her friends called Richard and Jane, it felt like things were falling into their rightful place.

And it felt right that Richard and Jane owned an old Victorian town house that they had converted into studio spaces, where they held yoga and Pilates classes. And it also felt right that no one hired the attic room in the house, because it was too small to hold a class in, but that didn't matter because the room had a large south-facing window, beautiful old floorboards and plain white plaster walls. And Jane said it had sunlight streaming in all day long.

And maybe life offered another step forward when they showed me the room and it was perfect and I loved it and Jane could tell that I loved it, and then I saw her whisper something to Richard, and when he nodded, she looked at me with a big smile on her face and said, "Would you like to use the room to paint in? It's not being used at the moment?"

"Really?"

"Yes, it's yours if you want it. No charge. I think you'll feel comfortable here, the room has such a peaceful feeling."

So even though Irene said that human beings seem hardwired

to see connections between things that don't really exist, in this instance, I felt they really did. And I believed that once I opened my heart up, made myself ready to paint, life had stepped in and provided me with everything I needed. Or perhaps it was always going to turn up, because that's what my life plan said would happen, along with brushes, acrylic paints, a blank artist's canvas and a tall wooden easel. The canvas a present from Janet, and the rest of the materials, a present from my Aunty Pat.

And when I started to paint, I had no idea what it would feel like, that the process of turning an image into clear expression would be so intense, so exhilarating that I'd never felt so alive. Right from the very first brush strokes, my thoughts and the brush connected and then we were no longer separate, the brush moving instinctively in small strokes, dabs, lines, over the textured surface of the canvas.

A flow started through my hand and my fingers and continued on into the wood of the brush and the bristles and paint, then something began to emerge on the canvas, something alive, communicating an idea and a feeling, something more than the paint and canvas, something that wasn't there before.

Layer upon layer of paint was applied, then moved around with the tip of the brush, then reapplied. First white, then reds, then yellows, then oranges and then white again, as the brush did its work, and something took over and became alive. Something inside me thrilled and marveled as the colors became more than just paint, and the paint took on a quality of living things and the colors became Beings of light and marble and shimmering blue cloth and dimensions of galaxies and entire universes, and above all, the Light of all light.

The midday sunlight was streaming in through the studio window, its warm rays bringing out the honey-rich glow of the oak floorboards and the chalky uneven surface of the white plaster walls. I made myself a mug of tea using the small portable kettle I'd been given and sat down at the wooden table to eat the carefully wrapped sandwiches I'd brought with me. The painting was now almost complete, even though my method of painting had been painfully slow because of my injuries and my inexperience. But it didn't matter, there was no hurry. Richard and Jane had already told me I could use the room for as long as I wanted to.

Fixing my gaze on the canvas, my eyes searched for any part of the scene that needed more color as I asked myself, for the hundredth time, whether it was finished or not. As I considered this question, I heard footsteps on the wooden studio stairs, then a soft, single knock on the door, and after a few seconds, the door creaked open and Richard and Jane walked in.

"Can we come in, we're dying to see it?" asked Jane, smiling.

"Please do," I said, getting up to wash my mug in the sink in the corner of the room, "although it's not finished yet."

They walked over and stood in front of the easel.

"Wow. That's amazing," said Richard.

"It's beautiful," said Jane, sighing deeply.

I smiled at them both, grateful for their enthusiasm and their support, and deep inside, I also felt the satisfaction of knowing that something in me had finally been released, a tension had unfurled itself, a process had finally clicked into place and their generous offer of the use of this studio space had helped create that possibility.

"People keep asking us what you're doing up here," said Richard. "Everyone's curious to know about your painting."

I knew that already, because if the door was open, I could hear the voices of the people from the yoga classes asking who was in the attic, then I'd hear Richard or Jane say, "It's David, our resident artist," then, "He's painting a picture of the afterlife. Yes, that's right. The afterlife. He had an accident and he went there. It was on the news. You must have seen it. Really fascinating story," then, "No, I don't think he'd mind if you popped up, just knock on the door first."

Of course I didn't mind. The appearance of people at the attic door did nothing to deter my focus, no matter what they said, or whatever pet theories they had about my near-death experience or their own versions of what it would be like to encounter the Afterlife. But then again, I had no idea, of all people, she would turn up.

Chapter 16

Universes Colliding

The studio door opened.

"You need to look after yourself," said Janet, walking in the room, carrying a small paper bag. The attic room suddenly smelled of freshly ground coffee. "You seem to be pushing it a bit."

"I'm fine," I said, ignoring the pain in my arm and legs, and trying my best not to limp too badly as I walked over to the table. I'd had enough of being treated like a glass vase that would break with the slightest physical exertion, and I had to stop myself being irritable with anyone who extended sympathy or offers of assistance.

Luckily, Janet didn't seem to notice as she reached in the bag, took out a small polystyrene cup and passed it to me. The smell of the fresh coffee really was delicious. Then she walked over to the painting, perched on the easel by the attic window, looked at it carefully and sighed.

"It's beautiful."

"Thanks. It's nearly finished now."

"How do you know what to paint?" she asked, tilting her head slightly to one side as though studying it from a different angle.

"It's like I have images in my head," I replied, trying to find the right words. "They feel so real and they build up, like a pressure and I have to get them out."

Janet took a deep breath, chewed her lip, then said, "I've started painting too."

"That's great," I replied, smiling. "It's about time you did something artistic. I've always thought you had a good eye."

"It's you who inspired me to do it. When you started doing

drawings of your near-death experience, I didn't think you'd keep it up. But when you stayed with us and kept on with the sketches, I saw how it filled you up and I guess I wanted a bit of that too. It dawned on me that I needed to step out of being a mother and a wife for a while and do something for myself."

"Can I see what you've done?"

"Not yet," she replied, a bit hesitantly. "I haven't shown anyone yet. But I will when I'm ready."

"Not even a little peek?" I said.

"No."

"Come on. Just one look?"

"No."

"What does Charlie think?"

"He says it's great, but I'm not going to show him anything either, he's far too critical," she said in mock exasperation. "Anyway, I have to go now, shopping to get."

"Thanks for the coffee," I called out, as she went out the attic doorway and started down the stairs. "And don't forget, I still want to see your painting."

"That's what Charlie says too," she called back, "but you'll both have to wait."

As I finished off the coffee, I heard her footsteps on the first-floor landing, then going down the stairs to the ground floor. A few seconds later, I heard the dull thud of the street door closing and for a while, the building was quiet again.

There was no sense of time passing as I became absorbed in my work, until I heard the sound of the church bells drifting in through the attic window. It was lunchtime now. Downstairs, people were coming and going from the yoga classes that ran throughout the day.

Voices in the hallways said hello or goodbye and doors closed again. Then, within a few minutes, the building fell silent again. It was as though the building had a regular rhythm throughout the day and I marked the passage of time by it.

In the silence of the now-settled building, I heard something that brought me out of my concentration and back into the real world. Footsteps on the wooden staircase that led up to the attic door. Someone was coming to see me.

"Hello," said a quiet polite voice outside the half-open doorway. "Is it okay to come in?"

"Yes, of course," I said. I was used to interruptions by now.

A tall, pretty girl with shoulder-length blond hair pushed open the door and came into the room. She was casually dressed, blue jeans, dark brown leather Chelsea boots and a white shirt worn loose over her trousers. Slung over her shoulder was a large, leather satchel, from which she pulled out a piece of paper.

"Hello, I'm Ariella. Jane and Richard said it would be okay to come up, they said you wouldn't mind. I hope it's okay?"

"Are you a painter too?"

"No, I'm a classical musician actually. Cellist. I play with the Chamber Orchestra of St. Ives."

"Sorry, not heard of them. Should I have?"

"No, not at all, not unless you like classical music," she said smiling. I noticed her gaze flicker over to where the easel was stood. "Is it okay to take a look?"

"Be my guest."

She walked over to the easel and stood in front of the painting for a few moments, her eyes wandering over the canvas. Then she took a couple of steps back, as though taking in a larger perspective. I got the impression she was familiar with appraising art but I guessed this was probably the first time she'd appraised a painting of the Afterlife.

"Jane and Richard said that you'd...had an accident," she said, hesitantly.

"Yes. I got pulled under a train," I replied. It was my stock answer these days.

"That must have been awful," she said, her eyes widening.

I didn't say anything. I couldn't bring myself to joke about it or pass it off lightly. It was still too uncomfortably real in my mind. After a few moments' silence, she spoke again.

"They also said you had some kind of experience afterwards…"

"I had a near-death experience if that's what you mean."

"I heard that," she said, an expression on her face which, if I had to describe it, I would say was a mixture between awe and curiosity.

"As you can probably guess, that's what the painting is about," I said, looking at the canvas.

"It must have been amazing," she said, her voice quieter now.

"It was. It changed everything."

"Everything?"

"Everything."

She looked at me as though she expected me to say something else, but I didn't. Then she looked momentarily nervous and I wondered if I'd come across as a bit abrupt, so I tried to explain things more clearly.

"Everything changed for me after my near-death experience. My whole world turned upside down. Before that, I was in a really bad way, but my life is better now. I see the world in a different way."

"A few years ago, I went through something that changed my life too," she said, and for a second, I caught a glimpse of sadness, an emotional echo that briefly surfaced on her face. "I was ill for a while and nothing the doctors did seemed to help. But then I saw an herbal therapist, and then everything got better for me. In fact, I was so impressed that I started training in herbal therapy treatments myself. That's why I'm here. I need people to act as case studies, and Richard and Jane suggested asking you." As her voice trailed off, she looked at me with a hopeful expression on her face.

"You want to give me herbs?" I asked, raising my eyebrows.

"Yes, if you don't mind?" she said, looking nervous again, as though she'd overstepped some invisible mark in the conversation. "They don't taste too bad and there aren't usually any side effects."

"You honestly think they'll help me recover from all this?" I said, looking down at my legs and my still barely moving left arm.

"Yes, I do," she said, her voice suddenly finding more confidence in its delivery.

I didn't know what to think. She seemed really genuine, and a small voice inside said what the heck, what have I got to lose, so I said I'd do it and she smiled warmly when I agreed.

"Great. Thanks. I'll leave you this questionnaire then," she said enthusiastically, offering me the piece of paper she'd been holding. "It's pretty self-explanatory, it just asks you some general questions about how you're doing, that kind of thing. I'll pick it up in a few days, then based on your responses, I'll make an herbal preparation for you and we'll meet every fortnight for a while, so that I can monitor your progress. How does that sound?"

"It sounds complicated," I said, but then I smiled as I'd already made up my mind to go for it. After all, what harm could a few herbs do that a train hadn't already done.

The next afternoon, I was so fully absorbed in painting the individual tiny stars that formed part of the waterfall of stars and galaxies on the left-hand side of the canvas, that I didn't consciously register the approaching sound of a vehicle whose exhaust was obviously in dire need of repair, drifting in through the attic window.

My neck was aching and my arm was stiff from holding the wooden artist's palette in my hand. The palette was heavy, but it gave me the time to work with each color before I applied it to the canvas. I could move the paint around on the wooden surface and mix different shades together to form a unique color. By now, it had become a piece of artwork in its own right to me, with its layers of colors built up from a random, messy patchwork of dried shades of paint lying across its surface, but I wasn't sure anyone else would see it like that.

I put the palette down on the table top, stretched my arm out and looked at the section of the canvas I'd just been working on. I could see it clearly now. The starlight needed more blue in it.

I rummaged around in the box of acrylic paint and found the tube of cobalt blue and squeezed out a large blob of liquid paint onto the palette surface. As I screwed the tiny lid of the paint tube back on, I became vaguely aware of voices on the floor below. Gruff voices, not the usual type of yoga client voices. Then I heard someone coming up the wooden attic stairs. From the heavy clump, clump, clump of footsteps, it sounded like an approaching army, definitely not the usual type of yoga client footsteps either. Then, someone opened the door and two people barged noisily into the room.

"Blimey. Look at you, Vincent Van Goffy," said Jimmy smiling broadly.

"Jimmy, Matt. What are you doing here?"

"We gotta see if the rumors are true," said Matt, shaking his head in mock concern.

"What rumors?"

"That you've lost the plot. Gone all arty."

"Do I look like I've lost the plot?" I said, holding my right arm out to reveal my paint-stained clothing.

They looked at each other, raised their eyebrows and nodded, solemnly.

"Yep," they said in unison.

I couldn't quite take in the image of Matt and Jimmy, stood here, in my studio. It was like two distinct universes colliding and my first reaction was to laugh aloud at the sight of the pair of them, looking awkward and out of place. I embraced them both, giving them a one-armed hug as best I could. I hadn't seen them since my first few days in hospital and that seemed like a lifetime ago now.

"We've been on a building site job in Cambridge, so thought we'd drop in to see you after work," said Jimmy, picking up one of my brushes, examining it carefully, then placing it back down again.

I could tell they'd been working on a site; their clothes were covered in the usual combination of sawdust, brick-dust and white emulsion paint. Matt walked over to look at the painting on the easel and Jimmy came over to the table and perched on the edge, next to me.

"Blimey. Is that what you reckon you saw then?" said Matt, shaking his head in what looked like sheer disbelief.

"Yep."

He tilted his head slightly to one side and pursed his lips and whistled. Then his eyebrows came together as he frowned, staring more closely at the painting. I'd seen that look on Matt's face before. It was his serious look. The one he did whenever Steve the bar manager asked difficult quiz questions.

"So, how are you doing then? After... all that," said Jimmy, as he looked at me out of the corner of his eye, then cocked his head in the direction of the painting. I assumed he was asking how I was, after falling under a train and visiting the afterlife.

"I'm okay. Not drinking any more though."

"Yeah, I heard. Steve says the bar takings are down by half."

Then his voice changed, and he looked at me with a serious expression, one I hadn't seen before. "You should have told us things were bad. We would have loaned you some money for your rent. You should have said something." He sounded a bit hurt as he said this.

"Yeah, I know. I'm sorry. You might have noticed by now, I'm not very good at asking for help," I replied, with a look on my face that said I knew he was right.

"We've figured that out for ourselves, mate. If you ever need to... you know you can... I mean... you don't have to... and if you don't want to, that's fine too..."

"Thanks, I really appreciate it," and I meant it too. I was touched. It meant a lot to me that he offered, and we stood there in silence for a few moments, still looking at the painting, steadfastly avoiding eye contact as most guys do when they are talking about anything personal or real.

"So... does it help then?" he asked, breaking the slightly tense silence. "Painting?"

"Yeah, it does."

"And you reckon you saw all that stuff?"

"Yeah. I did," I replied, trying to imagine how it must all seem to them. My painting, my near-death experience, my new life. We'd never touched on spiritual matters in the bar.

"The painting is brilliant, mate," said Jimmy. "But I've got to admit, I don't like that lot."

"Who?"

"The religious lot. Don't like them at all."

"It's not a religious painting, Jimmy, it has got nothing to do with religion," I said firmly, but Jimmy didn't seem to register this as he carried on with his train of thought that seemed to me to reveal something from his past that still carried a charge for him.

"It's how that lot use the idea of an afterlife that gets me," he went on, warming to his theme. "All them priests telling the poor to accept their lot in this life, because so long as they pray, they'll be rewarded in the next one. Opium for the masses to keep them quiet. That's what my dad used to say."

It was the first time I'd ever heard Jimmy sound so bitter, but I had to stand my ground, because I knew everything had changed for me, and even though my understanding of the change was new and raw and the strangeness of it too uncertain to describe, I wanted to make him understand, for me, it was the truth and it had nothing to do with priests or religion or politics.

"I know what I saw, Jimmy. I'm not the least bit religious, and I don't need a priest to be a go-between for what I felt in that place. I experienced it firsthand. That's what the painting is about. It's meant to show everyone what's waiting ahead for each and every one of us and we don't need anyone to act as a go-between to get to it."

Jimmy looked at me, chewed his lip, then smiled, the tension in his face evaporating as he did so.

"Well I hope your painting pays better than your old job. You sold any of them yet?"

"Nope. Not doing it to sell," I replied.

"Why are you spending all your time painting then?"

"Something got into me. I can't explain it, but I have to keep at it."

"Must be a nice feeling. I've never really known what I wanted to do in life. Not really. Wish I did," he said, glancing round the studio.

As he said this, Matt took a few steps backwards from the painting, still staring at it as though he was moving away from some ancient relic that he was afraid to turn his back on. After a few more backward steps, he bumped into the table edge at the opposite end to where we were perched. He groped blindly either side of him then, without looking behind, hoisted his large backside onto the table top, sitting right on top of the paint palette. I was just about to call out to stop him, but it was already too late. Jimmy shook his head and sighed.

After a few seconds, Matt jumped up from the table and started feeling around his backside with his hands, then stared with a horrified expression at the sight of his cobalt blue stained fingers.

"You sat on my paint palette," I explained, getting up from the table and trying hard not to laugh. "Don't worry, it'll come off in the wash."

I walked over to get the small hand towel I kept by the sink and soaked the corner of it under the cold tap and handed it to Jimmy, who looked at it in horror.

"Sorry, with my arm, it's a bit difficult, you'll have to get it off him," I said, throwing him my best innocent look.

Jimmy raised his eyebrows. "What are you worried about?" he said to Matt. "Your jeans are already covered in paint, they're your bloody work jeans."

Matt headed off downstairs to the bathroom on the second floor so that he could "have a proper look" at the "bloody stain". As we waited for him to return, Jimmy walked over to the painting and turned his back on me.

"By the way, I ran into Anna the other day," he said, lowering his voice and staring straight ahead at the painting.

"How is she?" I asked, suddenly aware of a strange sensation in the pit of my stomach.

"She's looking good."

"So... is she still going out with... that guy she met recently?" I had to ask. I couldn't help it. The question was still burning in the back of my mind, and it seemed that Jimmy was the one person who could answer it for me.

"I thought you didn't care?" he said, still avoiding eye contact.

"I don't," I lied.

"Sounds like it."

"I just want to know if she's happy?"

"If you are that interested, then why didn't you ask her out yourself when you had the chance?"

"I don't know," I said, truthfully.

"You really have no idea?"

"No. Not really."

"I'll tell you why you didn't. It's because you are a bloody idiot, that's why."

"Yeah, yeah." But I knew he was right. A few moments of silence passed, then I asked the one other question I couldn't get out of my mind. "So... are things going well... with her new boyfriend?"

"You want my advice? I reckon you missed your chance. You

need to move on."

"I take it that's a 'yes' then?"

I put the wet towel back in the sink and pushed the sleeve of my jumper up over my elbow, then remembered how scarred my arm was and quickly rolled the jumper back down again.

"Life doesn't always work out the way you want it to with everything in the right order," I said to myself as much as to Jimmy.

"Sorry, mate," he said, putting his hand on my shoulder. He was good like that, but I was in no hurry to seek another relationship, despite his next suggestion that I should think about "getting out and about again".

When the two of them eventually left, I had to laugh when I heard their run-down old car starting up outside the building. The bangs of the exhaust reminded me of old cartoons I watched as a kid, where comical characters would emerge from a very small car. A circus car. Trust Matt and Jimmy to have a circus car.

Over the next few months, the sun shone in through the attic window and the room felt like it had become a second home. I'd been painting for what seemed like forever now and yet the feeling that I still had things to do, things to sort out, was constantly there.

How far have I got to go with this?

I squeezed out a blob of green acrylic paint on to the wooden palette and tried to stretch out the ache in my neck and shoulders. Then another thought came to mind.

Look how far you have come.

With that thought, I turned and looked at the two finished paintings leant against the studio wall. Those paintings behind me were the culmination of the time I'd spent, here in this attic room, struggling to paint.

On the right, stood the NDE painting, as everyone called it

now. It was still my favorite. All the detail was there, the Beings of light, the grey slate, the liquid blue cloth and the tunnel of Light. The hardest part was trying to paint the quality of the swirling Light at my feet. But I did my best, and when I finished that part, I thought I'd captured it as best as I could.

On the left stood another painting, the one about the train accident itself. I'd given it the working title of *The Beauty Within*. The images for this one started coming when I'd nearly finished the NDE painting, and at first, it was hard to tell if they were just flashbacks about the accident, or whether they were something deeper, visions that were meant to be followed and turned into something else.

After a while, I realized the images had a different quality to the flashback episodes, and as time went on, they grew more vivid. Eventually, I couldn't get past them. They wouldn't let me pass. So I followed these new ideas faithfully and began to feel for their meaning and commit them to paint, and they ended up as the second painting. This one told the story of that day, feelings I couldn't explain to anyone in words, the raw emotions of the accident itself.

My arm was in the foreground of the scene, rising up from the bottom of the canvas. My raw, injured arm seemed both savage and wondrous at the same time, two distinct feelings tangled into one moment, when I lay on the track and saw all the nerves and muscles and bone that had been with me all my life, for the very first time.

Behind it, I'd painted a dark tidal wave sweeping upwards across the canvas, carrying me emotionally from the darkness of the oily track, swirling up, up into the heavenly blue of the Huntingdon station sky. It took me ages to get the color of the sky right. The cobalt blueness of it. I would never forget the blue of that sky. It said I'd made it. I'd survived. I was alive.

In the right-hand corner, I'd added the half-formed figure of a girl playing a cello, a ghostly imprint of an instrument with no strings and no bow. It felt to me as though it was a lament for the loss of my ability to play guitar, even though Ariella, who sat for me as a model for the imaginary figure a few weeks back, had probably never been near an electric guitar in her life. It didn't matter though, she posed with her cello and loved the image when I'd finished painting it.

Forcing myself back into the reality of my surroundings, I lowered the brush, took a few steps backward and sat on the edge of the little table for support. The room was illuminated by the bright sunlight and it was by this light that I gazed at my third painting.

This new one wouldn't need any explanation at all, at least that's what I told myself. It was a painting of the figure that came through during my first spiritual healing session with Joy. That's what I was working on now. The vision, just as I saw it, the one that released my creativity inside.

Lost in my own thoughts, I dipped the brush into a blob of brown acrylic paint I'd just squirted onto the palette, and was just about to apply a small stroke to the background of the figure when I heard footsteps on the wooden attic stairs, then the creak of the door opening and the sound of high heels echoing on the bare wooden floorboards of the room. Then a voice behind me spoke, and I turned around and saw the last person I would ever have expected to see again.

"Well, well, well. Quite the artist these days."

She took me completely by surprise. I could feel my heart rate quicken and became aware that I'd tensed up physically as I turned around to look at her and automatically tried to draw a deeper breath to ground myself. The relaxation technique Irene taught me to use whenever I felt under pressure.

"Hi," I replied. My mind went blank as I searched for something to tack onto the end of that sentence, but nothing came. Well, one thought did, but I wasn't going to say that particular one out loud. The question that ate away at me for months after we split. The question about whether she ever regretted dumping me for Adam?

I didn't move an inch, my body felt frozen to the spot being caught unawares like this. Then I realized that the brush I was holding had a watery blob of paint in the bristles that was beginning to form into a pendulous pear-shaped drop, so I grabbed a paper towel and wrapped it gently around the bristles so that I didn't get paint on the wooden floor.

Meanwhile, she confidently walked over to the paintings and stood in front of them, arms folded, head slightly tilted to one side, not saying a word as she unbuttoned her cashmere coat.

I couldn't see her face, but I could tell she was forming a quick snap judgement about the canvases. I'd seen the same look before when she used to look in the windows of expensive clothes shops, deciding whether to buy some outfit that cost more than one month's rent for my flat. Her judgements tended to be on the binary side. Yes, no, rich, poor, good or not good, that was about as subtle as I could remember them. After a few seconds of appraisal, she had obviously made her choice and she spoke as though we'd only just seen each other yesterday and nothing bad had ever happened.

"These are impressive. I never knew you had it in you."

"Thanks."

"I saw you on the television. On the news. Your accident."

"Oh."

For a few seconds, I weighed up how I felt at seeing her again as she flicked her shoulder-length blond hair over her shoulder. I had to admit, she was beautiful, even more so now and as she pretended to study the paintings, old stirrings of shame briefly welled up inside as memories of the disastrous dinner party surfaced. But its effect was feebler these days. I'd learned a lot since that night.

"How's Adam?" I couldn't help myself. I had to ask.

"Oh him. We split up ages ago. He went back to his wife."

"I didn't know he was still married."

"Neither did I," she said, sounding slightly bitter, but then she straightened up and her shoulders went back, but the gesture wasn't entirely convincing. For a moment, her confident stance wavered. "I don't work for him anymore," she continued, still clearly concealing a lingering rawness. "I've moved on. I work for an art dealer now, Sir Gerald Spencer-Right. Have you heard of him?"

"No."

"He's very well known in certain circles."

She paused and I wondered if she was waiting for me to react. I didn't say anything. Whatever she was doing here, I had no idea, but whatever her reason, I knew I had to keep my physical distance from her, no accidental contact, nothing.

Keep it formal and polite.

She spun around, and for a second, we just stared at each other and I thought I saw a flicker of nervousness across her face at my lack of response. It didn't stop her though; I knew she was tougher than that. She walked over to the wooden table, perched on the edge and carried on talking, and I could tell by the tone of her voice that she liked showing me her clever new insights into the art world.

"I've learned so much about the art business from him. Apparently, it's nothing to do with how good a painting is, it's all about the potential for investment returns. Gerald says that art is seen as a safer investment opportunity than the stock market these days and the art dealer's job is to create a market for a particular artist, wind investors up so they spend silly money on something that's just a bit of paint on canvas at the end of the day. Soft power he calls it. China is the big new marketplace. Gerald says it's taking over from the Russians and the Americans."

As she talked, random images of our relationship flashed through my mind. The lies about not fancying Adam. That horrible journey home from his mansion flat and the final, awful moment when she dumped me by text message...

"Are you listening?" I heard her say and my attention jumped back from old memories to the present moment in the room.

"Sorry, yeah, go on."

"As I was saying. Gerald's throwing a small party at a Soho gallery on Saturday to introduce a new artist he's taken on. He's so clever. He builds a story up around the artist, throws a small select party, invites the right investors. Makes them think that this is just what the market wants right now and that's all it takes. The artist sells their paintings and Gerald takes a big fat percentage of the sales price. It's all a bit of a game really."

She fiddled with something on the hem of her coat as she said this. I didn't say anything. I just watched her and concentrated on keeping my breathing steady. The smell of expensive perfume was strong now. Musk of some kind. Spicy. No doubt very expensive.

It was no good. The watery blob of acrylic paint on the tip of the brush I was holding was bleeding out of the paper towel and onto my hand, so I walked over to the small sink in the corner, turned on the cold water tap and put the brush tip in the running water. Brown-colored water spiraled down the white enamel and wound its way down the sink hole. The cold water felt good as it splashed on my hand, and as I spoke, I kept my focus on the spiral of water.

"It's good you're putting your art degree to use."

"I'm surprised you remembered that," she said.

I didn't reply, so she got up from the table, adjusted the collar of her coat then opened her shoulder bag. Reaching inside, she pulled out a small card, which she placed on the little wooden table and said, "Here's my number, I've got a new place, just off the King's Road."

She seemed like she was waiting for me to say something back. But I still didn't say anything. I just looked at her as she started walking towards the attic door.

"So, let me know if you fancy coming," she said.

"Coming?"

"On Saturday night. Gerald's party. I could introduce you if you like."

She pulled her coat around her and began buttoning it up, sending me a signal, telling me that time was running out; if I wanted what she was offering I had to say something because there would be no going back from this moment.

As I looked at her, stood in the doorway, I became aware of a long-forgotten ache inside my chest, a ghost of a physical, visceral pain, the remnants of the depression I'd felt towards the end of our relationship. Then I thought of the hard-won self-knowledge it had given me and Joy's words came to mind, about how my relationship with Emily might have been exactly what I needed to experience at the time. Although I had no idea what lesson I might have been part of for her life plan, she certainly didn't seem changed in any way I could recognize.

As I thought all this, she gazed at me curiously and my thoughts must have shown because there was now a trace of impatience in her voice.

"Maybe see you on Saturday then."

And with that, she walked out of the studio and I heard the sound of her heels clicking on the wooden steps down to the next floor and then all the way out of the building, till the heavy street door shut with a thud. I sat down at the table and started to dab the brush tip gently to make sure it was back to its normal shape as it dried, a tip I'd learned from a painter and decorator on a building site.

Emily's card was still lying on the table where she'd left it, and eventually my eyes glanced towards it, almost against my own will.

Fine embossed lettering, elegant script, an address in Chelsea, landline and mobile number and a list of small logos, e-mail, Twitter, Facebook, Flickr, with names or links beside each one. I looked at it for several seconds, trying to process the information, realizing what kind of world it represented. A world I'd briefly got to know through Emily more than I ever meant or wanted to know, a world I had no interest or intention of inhabiting anymore.

It was obvious what needed doing. I picked up the card and carefully ripped it into small pieces and threw it in the wastepaper basket by the sink.

Deep breathing, it seemed, had finally worked.

Chapter 17

Play the Five Tones

It was well after 7pm by the time I got to the Spiritualist Church. Tidying up at the studio after Emily's visit had made me arrive later than usual, but the by-now familiar elderly man sat behind the front desk smiled and reassured me that one of the healers was free and there was, in fact, still enough time for a healing before tonight's session ended.

The brisk walk from the studio to the hall had taken its toll, my leg was aching badly and I was still slightly out of breath as he quietly opened the wooden double doors and led me into the main room. Thankfully, Joy was free, waiting in the far corner, an empty chair beside her.

"Just be open to what happens," she said, as I sat down and she settled her hands gently on my shoulders.

I nodded, grateful that it was Joy doing the healing.

"Then I'll begin," she replied, her healing voice as warm and comforting as silk, and once more, I closed my eyes and waited for the peaceful feeling to take over.

At first, images of Emily flickered through my mind; I couldn't help myself, the impact of her visit to the studio was still reeling through me. But eventually, after a few minutes, a soft, silent curtain of blackness descended over my conscious thoughts and the deeper part of me let go into the warmth and familiarity of the quiet, still peace inside.

In that stillness, in the soft darkness of my mind's eye, it was as though ghostly, transparent images came floating towards me and I was watching them from a great height, like a bird soaring through the sky looking dreamily down to the Earth below. I lost myself in the feeling until I heard Joy's soft voice in my ear, pulling me back into focus.

"We are coming to the end of the session now. I want you to stretch out your fingers and toes and begin to feel yourself back in the room. That's it. Start stretching. Gently now. Open your eyes when you feel ready."

When I opened my eyes, she was stood in front of my chair, hands gently clasped together.

"How do you feel?" she asked.

"Relaxed. Very peaceful," I replied, struggling for a few minutes to come back from the immersive quietness I'd felt within.

"Good. I think it was a powerful session for you, the energy flowing through me felt unusually strong."

That comment moved me to ask the question that had been hanging around half-formed in the back of my mind for some time now, even though the healing session was coming to an end and people had started to pack away the other chairs.

"Can I ask you something? Have we got time?"

"Of course," she said smiling, "fire away."

"Do you have any idea why I was sent back?" I said, trying to stretch out my legs, which by now were feeling very stiff.

"What do you mean?"

"Well, at first I thought it was to do the paintings. I thought once I'd finished them, that would be it, I'd feel like the job was done. But I don't. There's something else I'm supposed to do. I can feel it, I feel it all the time, but I don't what it is. Do you have any idea what it is?"

She took a long, slow breath and raised her eyes upwards, as though drawing inspiration from somewhere else.

"Don't look for an answer immediately. Be okay with the journey itself and don't worry how it's going to unfold. Just concentrate on creating the conditions in your life where the magic can show up, then your faith will become like a flowing river, carrying you exactly where you need to go, showing you exactly what you need to do. Then, at the right time, if you pay attention, there will be a sign. You will notice things beyond mere coincidence, people may cross your path or say unexpected words that have a deeper meaning for you and you will know it when it happens."

"How?"

"You will feel it with your body."

"Like a hunch you mean?"

"In a way, although a hunch can be unreliable, especially when the mind tries to interfere with its real meaning. But a true sign, when it comes, will feel much stronger, as though you have finally remembered something you had long forgotten."

The look of puzzlement on my face must have showed, so she tried explaining it another way.

"Have you ever gone shopping for something you needed, and when you got to the shop, you couldn't remember what it was you went for?"

I thought hard for a moment, then such a memory surfaced.

"Yes."

"And can you remember how you racked your brains, trying to recall the thing you wanted and the feeling of frustration when you couldn't bring it to mind?" she prompted.

I nodded. I remembered a time when I'd walked all the way up Highgate Hill to get to the local supermarket, and by the time I'd got there, I'd forgotten what it was I went to buy. I could still recall how frustrated I felt, looking at the shelves, trying to remember what it was.

"Good," she said, watching me carefully. "Now, recall the moment where you finally remembered what it was you went for. What did you feel, inside?"

I pictured myself back in that moment when the uncomfortable uneasiness of not remembering was suddenly, instantly transformed.

"It was like something physical released, deep inside," I said.

"Exactly," she said excitedly. "The relief of remembering that which you have forgotten. A sign will feel similar. The part of you that already lives in Spirit will attempt to bring a sign to your conscious awareness at the right time when the fork in the road comes, and if you are awake to it, you will feel a similar sense of tension, an uneasiness, something being communicated beyond words, urging you at that moment to make the right choice, take the right path at the fork. When you do, the feeling of profound, internal release will be unmistakable, and you will know it when it happens. Then, your way ahead will become apparent. All you have to do is to be open to the mystery and flow of faith—"

She stopped speaking suddenly, and as I watched her face, something in her changed, her eyes became more intense, like deeper pools that led somewhere mysterious; and as if someone else was speaking through her, she then spoke in a voice that did not sound like her own, with such strange power and strength of quality in its delivery, it made the hairs on the back of my neck stand on end as I listened.

"Why am I seeing a violin placed across your chest? And I'm hearing Wagner. Beethoven. I'm hearing their music in my head... Oh... now I understand. They are telling me that you are going to write a piece of music. This music will be about your near-death experience. They tell me that you will be guided in this. They say that a lot of people are going to hear it... Yes... that's what they are saying... a lot of people will hear this music... Does this make any sense to you?"

"No... it doesn't," I said, "sorry."

I'd never bothered telling Joy I used to play in punk bands when I was younger, there didn't seem to be any point, especially now I couldn't play guitar again. But she ignored the puzzled look on my face and in the same strange, powerful voice, whispered the last bit of the message in my ear.

"They are saying, it's time for you to begin."

And as she spoke these words, it was as though a boundary

had been crossed somewhere deep inside, something came forward and moved through me, to make itself known, and part of me felt as though I had been expecting it.

The High Street was packed this morning, everyone wearing the same focused expression as they hurried in and out of the shops, but thankfully, the coffee shop didn't look too busy, so I decided to go in.

"Small cappuccino, please."

The voice of Amy Winehouse drifted out of the radio behind the counter as the bored barista took my money and handed me my coffee. As I walked over to sit at the empty table by the window, I picked up a magazine from the rack on the wall. Reading was still a real chore, but I had 35 minutes to kill before my appointment with Irene, and this magazine had a lot of photos.

After skimming through the pages, for want of something else to do, I slowly stirred the powered chocolate sprinkles into the cappuccino froth and looked out of the cafe window at the High Street outside. A young couple walked past and peered in through the window. He was holding her hand and the way he glanced at her and the softness of their faces as they talked to each other made me think of Anna, and then, as if by unconscious habit at the very thought of her these days, an involuntary, deep sigh emerged.

I managed to make the coffee last another fifteen minutes until the only thing left was a blob of milky-brown-colored foam sat at the bottom of the cup, but it did its job of killing time, and with five minutes left, I got up, returned the magazine to the rack, left the cafe and walked the short distance along the busy street to Irene's first-floor office, its street door next to a newsagent's shop.

"So? How are you today?" asked Irene, as we both made ourselves comfortable in our usual chairs, her expression carefully neutral, as it always was at the beginning of a session.

"I'm doing okay, thanks."

"And how are the paintings coming along?"

"Finished the most recent one a couple of weeks ago. I've done seven now."

"That's quite incredible," she said, shaking her head as though slightly mystified by what she was hearing. "You've come on such a long way since our first meeting."

"Thanks," I said, fighting an urge to look away out of embarrassment. "It's a funny feeling to have people saying well done, I'm not used to it."

She smiled then leaned back in her chair, settling herself into a comfortable position with her hands clasped in her lap, resting on her notebook. That was the signal to say the serious work was about to start, I knew all the signs by now.

"So, today, I thought we could talk about Anna."

"Anna?" I said, aware that I'd been caught off guard, and unable to hide the defensive tone in my voice.

"Yes. This will help us to look more deeply into your fear of reaching for things you want in a relationship."

I couldn't think of how to respond and I couldn't help wishing that she hadn't started the session on this particular topic, of all things.

"Do you still think about her?" she pressed, breaking the silence.

"Not really," I lied, even though I knew she could probably see right through my defense. "Anyway," I added, shrugging my shoulders, "Jimmy told me she's going out with someone else now."

"And how do you feel about that?"

"She's moved on. What can I feel?"

"Sad? Upset? Angry?"

"It doesn't matter what I feel. It's too late."

"But it does matter, because talking about it could help reveal hidden beliefs that still drive certain behaviors in you."

"Such as?"

"Believing you will never be good enough for someone, just as you are," she said, and in that half-space between moments, I was back in the bedroom of my Highgate flat the night after the terrible dinner party, hating myself for messing everything up. "So today, I think it would help if we talked about what you want out of a relationship," she continued.

Suddenly I felt cornered and my gaze slid along the row of framed certificates by the bookcase as I looked for a way out, an escape from this topic, but Irene waited for a response, and in the end, I had to say something.

"I can't deal with a relationship right now. It's too hard."

"What do you mean?"

"Having a relationship. I can't do it. It's okay seeing someone for a date and things go well and you are both on your best behavior and she doesn't get to see all the things about you that are bad because you are very careful to keep that stuff well hidden. But if things got out of hand..."

"Out of hand?" she repeated, looking puzzled. "I don't understand?"

"If I ask her out, I'm committing to something and then she'll want me to stay over and then we'll be sleeping together and spending time together and then she gets to see who I really am and..." my voice faded so Irene finished off my sentence.

"And then she doesn't like you anymore?"

"Something like that," I said, sighing deeply.

"Listen to me. I've seen a lot of successful clients in my time. Women and men from all walks of life. Lawyers, bankers, businessmen and women, all high achievers in their field. But do you know why they all come to see me? What they all have in common?"

"What?" I said, still gazing at the framed certificates on the wall.

"They can't find the same level of success in their own personal lives, because a lot of them put all their energies into their work. They feel safer that way."

"I don't understand?"

"When you've been doing this job as long as I have, you realize something. People come here, they all have their own story and each story has its own individual details. But on the whole, peel away the detail, and you get the same basic issue time and time again, which is that most of us are afraid to love. To fully commit to loving another human being, and in the process, to let that other person inside our defenses, our armor, to see who we really are, warts and all, because it takes real courage to love. The people who turn up at my office are full of courage, but most of them got hurt somewhere along the line. Maybe their mum didn't love them enough. Or their father was too strict or too angry, or he never came home. The trouble is, once we get hurt for the first time, we find ways to protect ourselves from being hurt again and that defense takes over and that's when the problems really start."

"I didn't want to mess things up with Anna."

"Of course, you didn't. In fact, it seems to me that you had and still continue to have strong feelings for her," she said. "At the time, I believe you felt you needed to protect yourself from taking on any more hurt, but in the process, you've stopped yourself from being able to connect with what you really feel inside. I believe that's why you couldn't face opening up to Anna, because if you did, you would have to open up to your own pain."

We sat there in silence for a few moments as I absorbed her words. Then another bad thought surfaced and I gave voice to it.

"Anyway, I'm not sure it's worth the effort."

"What isn't?"

"A relationship."

"I hear that a lot these days," she said, taking off her glasses to rub the bridge of her nose between her fingers, "mostly from people who are unhappy with their partner but aren't prepared to try to change themselves, they just want the other person to change."

"I wasn't expecting Anna to change," I argued back. "It was my fault that things didn't work out between us, not hers."

"And what about Emily? Did you want her to change?"

"I don't know? Maybe. Although with her it was all about the money."

"Really? You think so?"

As she challenged me like this, the strange thing was, it actually felt like a relief to be finally talking about my relationships, exposing them to the light of day, finding a chink of hope that I might finally get to understand how to love someone and be loved back. So when she then asked me to close my eyes and lean back in my chair to make myself more comfortable, I did.

"Good," she said, in a softer, quieter voice. "Now I want you to do something for me. I want you to imagine a couple."

"A couple?"

"Yes, a couple. Having a relationship together. Go along with me here."

"Okay. A couple," I repeated, picturing two random people in my mind.

"Now. I want you to imagine he's the third child of a poor family. Always got the hand-me-downs or the smallest portions or the least affection when he was growing up. Never enough left by the time it got to his turn. Now he's a big boy, he works hard at his job, long hours every day, because one lesson he learned in life, you've got to work hard to get enough, whatever it is, security, safety, love."

"And the girl?" I asked, drawn into the story almost against my own will.

"She comes from a well-off family. Got everything she wanted as a kid. But Daddy's a hard-working man, stays late at the office every day. So, she got everything she wanted as a child whenever she wanted it, except the one thing she wanted the most. Her father's love."

"Okay, I get the picture," I said. "Rich girl wants Daddy to pay attention to her, poor boy wants to finally get his fair share in life without having to kill himself working for it. So?"

"So, imagine this couple meet, fall in love and end up living together. One day, in the weekly shop, they buy a bag of chocolate chip cookies. Not cheap ones though, these are handmade expensive ones. Then two days later, the guy is working late as usual and by the time he gets home, he's looking forward to having a couple of those hand-made cookies, but she's already eaten the whole lot. When he realizes this, they have a big row. He says she's selfish. She's hurt and angry, because she doesn't understand why he's so upset about a few chocolate cookies."

"Personally, I'd have been pretty upset too," I replied, instinctively siding with the guy with no money.

"The point is," said Irene, "is the row really about the cookies, or is it about something far deeper?"

"Like what?" I asked, as a memory flashed into my mind of the night I first met Anna and she said something similar when I told her about splitting up from Emily.

"Maybe he is really saying, as a kid, there was never enough left for me, I never felt good enough and now it's starting again, I'll never get my fair share, no matter how hard I try. And maybe she just takes the cookies for granted because she never had to worry about having enough as a kid. But what she is really saying is, please don't let me down too."

"Are you saying that I failed at keeping up with Emily's expectations because I wasn't loved in the way I wanted to be when I was growing up?" I said, opening my eyes.

"I'm trying to show you that a lot of what passes for love isn't love at all, it's just older stuff working itself out in a relationship, blocking the real love out."

"Try telling Emily that. Nothing I ever did for her was good enough," I said bitterly.

"It must have been exhausting," she replied, "not speaking your truth and secretly trying to please her all the time."

When she said this, I felt a stab of painful recognition and shifted slightly in my chair to cover it up.

"The thing is," she continued, "if you exhaust yourself through trying to love someone else by trying to please them, you are not giving real love, it's a form of manipulation disguised as real love. Most of us get caught up in doing it at one time or another. You give your effort to that person because you are trying desperately to get their love to feel good about yourself, but you don't speak your truth because you are afraid they will walk away if you do. Only the other person doesn't know any of this, so they just keep taking whatever effort you are giving and not realizing you have unmet needs of your own. But the minute we actually love someone with no strings attached, that's when everything gets healthier. That's what real love is."

"Maybe," I said half-reluctantly, but I knew there was a great deal of truth in her words. Several moments went by and the two of us sat in a strange kind of comfortable silence. I got the impression Irene was creating a space in me, letting her words have the time they needed to settle somewhere inside. When she spoke again, her voice was soft and her tone even kinder.

"Listen to me. You're not the only person who's afraid of love. Far from it. But I really believe a good life, full of love, is possible for you. I'm sure of it, but only if you don't shy away from the challenge."

I felt mildly cheerful at her words yet conflicted too. On one hand, her encouragement touched an invisible thread of hope and thoughts of Anna flashed into my mind, but no sooner had I imagined the possibility of a relationship when another thought took hold and a voice whispered, "Not yet." It felt as though some strange force of will took the idea of Anna away and tucked it somewhere deep inside, because that same force of will that had led me to paint had something else in mind for me at this time.

How would I explain this strange conflict to Irene, I wondered? I didn't worry about disappointing her, this wasn't like family relationships or friendships. Our conversations were free and unencumbered, and I had absolute trust in her because of that, even if she didn't believe in anything that couldn't be backed up with a stack of scientific papers. But this wasn't going to be easy. I had no time to mentally rehearse what I was going to say, so I just said the first words that came to mind.

"I hear what you say, and I promise I'll think about it, but there's one more thing I need to do before I try to have a relationship."

"And what's that?" she said, looking curious.

"I don't know yet. I'm waiting for a sign."

"A sign?" she repeatedly slowly.

"Yeah. A sign. From Spirit."

"Let me get this straight," she said, tilting her head to one side as though studying my face from a slightly different angle. "You think there is something else you are supposed to do, as a direct result of your near-death experience?"

I nodded. "Yes. I do."

"And you feel compelled to do this thing, even though you don't know what it is yet?"

"Yes."

She paused for a second, as though taken aback and I gathered from her tone of voice that this was an unexpected turn of events.

"But your paintings? You've already achieved so much. Isn't that enough? Are you sure you're not focusing on your creative work as a way of avoiding a relationship?"

"No. There's more to do, I can feel it," I insisted truthfully. "I just have to wait until I get a sign. Then I'll know what I'm supposed to do in the future."

Her eyes widened slightly but I'd underestimated her tenacity and she caught me off guard as she changed tack, her tone now carefully neutral as she talked.

"I went to see a tarot card reader once, at a funfair, just for a bit of fun. This was in the days when I was a bio-medical research scientist. That was my life then, research. I had no idea I was going to change careers and become a psychotherapist later on. Anyway, this tarot card reader told me to shuffle the deck of cards he laid out on the table, then cut them into little piles. As I did this, he switched on a little tape recorder he had on the table and said he was going to record the session and give me the tape afterwards, so that I could listen back to it later.

"He then laid the cards out on the table in the shape of a Celtic Cross and told me that the position of each card had certain significance. For the rest of the session, he went through each card, one by one, and depending on what the card picture denoted, told me what my future would be. He talked so fast as he flipped each card over in turn, that when I left, I could only recall two things he'd said during the whole session.

"The first was that I currently worked in 'a science lab', as he called it. I have to admit, that was impressive. The second thing he said was that I'd change careers in a few years. He was adamant about this, he said the cards were giving him a clear sign that this would happen, and he pointed to two cards in particular. One was called 'The Counsellor' and the other one, 'Guardian Angel'. He said the position of these two cards showed that I would work as a counsellor in the future. Apart from those two things, everything else he'd predicted was recorded on the little cassette tape that he gave me at the end of the session. And do you know what I did with that tape?"

"No. What?" I said, my curiosity piqued.

"I threw it in the nearest bin outside."

"Why?"

"I didn't want someone to tell me what they thought lay

ahead, because then I'd never know if it was just a self-fulfilling prophesy if I became what they predicted. To this day, I'm not sure whether I became a psychotherapist because he planted the idea in my head in the first place or whether I would have eventually chosen this career path regardless. Whatever the reason, I certainly don't think it was because of any grand destiny or fate."

"In other words, you think the medium planted the idea of an accident in my head and I fell under a train to make it a self-fulfilling prophecy," I argued back, feeling vaguely offended.

"No, not at all," she said in a reassuring tone. "I just want you to stop for a moment and consider the rational alternative, that's all. I'm not dismissing what you believe, but as I've said before, human beings seem hardwired to see connections between unrelated coincidences, especially if it aligns with something they already want or fear."

"So you think it's crazy, waiting for a sign?"

She paused for a moment, sat back in her chair and glanced over at her bookcase, as though drawing wisdom from some unseen source.

"Some people would say no, it's not," she said carefully. "In fact, there are some that might envy you for it. Such a feeling can give a person a sense of purpose and meaning to their life. That's a rare thing."

For a few moments, neither of us said anything, we just looked at each other, then Irene broke the silence.

"Do you have any idea what form this sign will take or where it might lead you?"

"No, none."

"Then how will you recognize it?"

"I don't know. I just will, when the time comes..."

After the session had finished, I felt quite tired. My arm was beginning to ache and my legs felt stiff; I'd overdone it the past few hours, walking into town for my appointment, then walking all the way home again, and it was a relief to ease myself into bed a few hours later.

There was a bright full moon in the night sky, and when I switched off the bedside lamp, the moonlight through the window cast strange grey shadows over the bedroom furniture. Everything seemed quiet and still, and I made myself comfortable, ready to start doing the relaxation techniques. Nothing too complicated, just some deep breathing exercises Irene had taught me to help with the post-traumatic stress and pain. The aim was to empty my mind of any emotion or thoughts, and to get my body to relax before going to sleep. That was the general idea.

In... hold breath for 5 seconds... and out... in for 5... and out...

Behind my closed eyes, a deeper darkness took over the ghostly curtain of moonlight as conscious awareness lessened its hold. Most nights, I didn't even reach the end of the deep breathing routine before falling asleep. But tonight, as I started relaxing to the gentle movement of my breath, I heard something quite distinct from the sound of my own breathing. A series of musical notes, a melody. As plain as day.

All my senses were suddenly on high alert and my skin prickled. I opened my eyes and held my breath, and listened with every fiber of my being in the moonlit darkness of the room; but there was only silence.

I must have imagined it.

And then, there it was again.

A phrase of music.

It was as though it was breathed inside my head, like a ghostly whisper coming forward from a distant land, crossing a strange, imperceptible border to fall somewhere inside the deepest part of my awareness. A phrase of music. I was sure of it.

I listened for a while longer, staring into the shadows of the moonlit room. The music wasn't like an unwelcome presence and it didn't feel like I had someone intruding in my head. The sensation was different from that. It was like hearing something intimately familiar, coming from an unknown half-remembered world deep inside.

I couldn't recognize the melody, but the plaintive sequence of notes moved me, and I tried to commit the phrase to memory as my eyelids started to become heavy and tiredness overwhelmed my body.

The next thing I remember was waking up, sunlight streaming into the bedroom and the first thing that came to mind was whether I could remember the phrase or not.

I lay still for a few seconds and searched through my memory of the night before and heaved a big sigh of relief. It was still there. I could sing through the melody in my head.

Chapter 18

Ariella's Invitation

If there was such a thing as synchronicity, then Janet's arrival at my flat later that morning seemed beyond mere coincidence, offering the perfect opportunity to sort out my next few steps. She had brought coffee and croissants, and even though I was struggling to contain my excitement, my hunger felt a huge wave of affection for her as I drank the cappuccino and took mouthfuls of buttery dough in-between sentences where I explained what had happened the previous night.

"Well, what do you think?" I asked, after swallowing the last bit of the delicious warm croissant, feeling distinctly cheerful.

Janet turned slowly where she stood, to face me. She had been looking out of my window at the river flowing by below, taking in what I'd just said.

"Let me get this straight. You've been hearing music?" she asked, looking slightly concerned, which, in retrospect, wasn't all that surprising.

"Yes. And I need to find a way to record it," I replied, licking the remaining melted butter off my fingers, still relieved that I had a clear memory of the plaintive phrase of music even though it was hours ago when I first heard it.

"Would I know it?" she said. "Was it a hit?"

"No. I don't think it's someone else's music. I think it's meant to be mine."

A few days later, both of us stood looking at two large and dusty cardboard boxes balanced on the desk in my flat. The first box literally fell apart as we took the lid off between us. It hadn't been easy, getting the two boxes down from Janet and Charlie's garage attic, especially as I still couldn't use my injured arm very well. But at least Charlie hadn't thrown them away during one of his regular clear-outs. Janet said he cleared things out a lot and she reckoned it was probably the logical side of his brain looking for order in the home. I was clearly nothing like Charlie.

The plastic synthesizer still looked the same as I remembered it. I'd bought it years ago, when I formed my first band. At the time, I was more interested in my guitar and not that interested in learning to play keyboards, so the unloved and barely-used synthesizer ended up in storage in Janet's attic ever since. I had no recollection of how it ended up there, but Janet said I left it there because I thought her boys might like it when they got older.

At the time, neither of us had any idea how much technology would move on, so it was no surprise that when Janet's sons were old enough to be interested in making music, they laughed when they saw the dated plastic synthesizer, and downloaded a keyboard emulator software app instead.

Even I had to admit, as we pulled off the polystyrene protective packaging, the red and black plastic casing looked ancient. But it didn't matter, because it had some built-in orchestral sounds which meant I could flick a switch and the synthesizer would sound just like a violin, or a horn, or a piano. At least that was what the description on the box lid said.

Once I'd found the mains lead, plugged it in and located the on/off switch, the little display screen flashed into life and three promising words appeared in flickering green lettering on a dull-grey backlit background.

Ready to play.

We both listened very carefully when I selected the sampled sound entitled 'Violin' and played random notes on the keyboard. When I stopped playing and the last note died out, I looked at Janet to see what she thought.

"It's terrible," she said, "it sounds more like a Fisher-Price toy than a violin."

"It's not that bad," I said, half-heartedly.

"It's terrible."

She was right, it was, but I felt strangely excited and cheerful at the prospect of having a way to play music once more. Now all I needed was something to record the music with.

Charlie didn't believe in mystical things such as hearing music out of the blue, but he was, as usual, helpful when Janet told him I needed something I could record music with. Two days later, Janet dropped by again, this time bringing with her an expensive-looking digital voice recording device.

"Are you sure Charlie doesn't use it anymore?" I said, examining it.

"I'm sure. He bought this when it first came out, but he's got the newer model now."

"Why doesn't that surprise me."

"Good luck," she said, smiling, heading off towards Charlie and home. "I hope it all works."

The English translation of the Japanese voice recorder operating manual wasn't exactly dyslexia-friendly, and it took me some time to figure out how to work the stop, play and record functions. Once I'd got that mastered, I started to get to grips with the synthesizer.

Playing a one-fingered melody that sounded like a strangled, tinny violin on the plastic keyboard was the easy part. Anyone with a musical ear enough to remember a melody could master that. However, trying to figure out how to get the voice recorder to record at the same time was another level of physical effort entirely, especially when my injured left arm started to ache really badly, pushed to its limits from holding down the Record button with my left hand as I played the sequence of notes with my right one.

Nevertheless, slowly, something recognizable began to take shape as I recorded the melody, note by note, until finally, as the sun started to set over the River Great Ouse outside my window, I pressed the Play button on the voice recorder to listen to what

I'd recorded, and a strange shiver ran down the back of my spine as I did.

I laid the device down carefully on the desk beside the synthesizer and looked out at the sky beyond the window. Something had unlocked in me; I hadn't expected it to be there, but it was, and the idea came to me that the phrase of music I had just listened to might be a fragment of a much larger piece...

Over the next few days, in between the mundane routine of daily life, washing and ironing clothes, cooking, walking to the shops, meeting Janet for coffee in town, the quiet solitude of my flat became increasingly valuable; the synthesizer was left out on the desk, plugged in, ready to come alive at the switch of a button, the voice recorder fully charged, everything ready in case more inspiration appeared out of the blue.

It wasn't as though I was willing myself to compose, in fact, if I tried to force it, nothing came. It was only when I felt relaxed, or was falling asleep, or waking up, or preoccupied with a mundane task such as washing up, or gazing out the window or cooking, that a melody would pop into my head, fully formed. Then I'd switch on the synthesizer and play the melody, one note at a time, so that I could record it.

At first, it felt like a small tear seemed to have been made in some invisible veil, and initially, like a trickle of water, small drops started dripping through. Then, as though the gap were widening, more lines of melody started to flow.

Soon, they began to get more complex, the parts more involved and the sounds in my head became not just one instrument, but several. It could only mean one thing. I was hearing additional parts. This wasn't just a solo melody; it was part of something involving far more than just one instrument, and as I realized this, I began to wonder if this music was the beginning of a much bigger piece of music altogether.

Some of the instruments I heard in my imagination, such as piano and violin, were relatively easy to recognize, and I knew the sound of a French horn from Ian's relentless childhood practice of it after school. But other instruments were a complete mystery and linking a part played in my head with the right instrument on the synthesizer became more and more time consuming.

It didn't matter though. With the freedom to slowly record each part in whatever way I wanted, my lack of musical knowledge made no difference to the sense of fulfilment and satisfaction I felt when I listened back to the day's recordings, because the sense of waiting was over. On some deeper level, I felt a sense of release, knowing I was doing what I was meant to be doing and it was all I wanted to do, to hear it all out loud, outside my head, for real. That was all I wanted. Nothing more.

The traffic on the St. Ives High Street was already snarled in the lunchtime rush hour as I made my way to meet Ariella. I felt tired and my arm was sore, so I looked forward to the imaginary cappuccino I'd already formed a picture of in my mind, steaming hot with the creamy froth lightly dusted with a sprinkling of chocolate powder.

By the time I arrived at the cafe, she was already waiting at the usual table, ready to ask me a series of questions and make notes of my answers, so that she could prescribe her latest herbal remedy preparation for me.

"Was I sleeping well? How did I feel emotionally?" These were slightly uncomfortable questions I usually did my best to avoid answering, but after greeting her and ordering two cappuccinos at the counter, I let myself be studied once more.

"How are you?" she asked, like she always did when she was about to write up her latest herbal treatment case notes on her patient who went under a train and visited the afterlife.

"I'm okay, thanks," I said, trying to read the upside-down writing in her notepad and doing my best to be as honest as possible without going into too much detail, especially as the cafe was busy and people were sat nearby, half-listening in on the conversation.

It wasn't as easy talking to someone nearer my own age as it was talking to Irene or Joy, so I kept my answers vague, then changed the subject and asked her questions about the orchestra she played in, or how her herbal training course was going. But she was determined and quickly steered the conversation back to my mental and physical recovery.

After I'd explained that, "Yes, I felt good," and, "Yes, I was sleeping well," and, "No, nothing is bothering me at the moment," she studied my face carefully, squinting slightly as she concentrated, as though trying to see what lay behind my responses and whether the truth of my inner condition tallied with what I presented on the outside.

As she peered even closer, the waiter came over to give the laminate table top a cursory wipe, then brought over two freshly-made cappuccinos, and I couldn't help noticing the slightly puzzled look on his face as he placed them down on the table in front of us. It must have looked strange to anyone watching, me quietly cringing as I attempted to look at nothing in particular whilst Ariella peered closely at my face, confirming to anyone interested that her amateur status meant she was still fairly slow at facial diagnosis.

But despite the awkwardness of being stared at and examined in a public place, I still felt a sense of obligation to answer her questions as honestly as possible because I couldn't help feeling a kind of kinship with her; we'd both developed faith in things that were definitely outside the mainstream.

"I think I'll add some White Willow Bark and Turmeric into this month's treatment," she said, more to herself than to me as she moved her coffee cup aside and opened up her leather satchel on the cafe table so that she could take out various tiny bottles of raw herbal ingredients, ready to prepare my latest prescribed remedy.

I watched her as her eyes wandered over the row of bottles and thought about the half-dozen times we had met up since that day in the attic studio and how she'd enjoyed acting as a visual reference for the imaginary cello player in my painting about the accident. Since then, several herbal potions had come my way and I'd taken them all, like the good test subject I was. Ariella seemed pleased with my progress, and in whatever way herbal remedies were supposed to be of help, apparently, I'd passed all the markers.

"So, are you keeping busy at the moment?" she asked, as she began unscrewing the lid of a tiny bottle. She looked preoccupied and I could tell the conversation had moved into polite pleasantries to fill time as she began mixing the various herbal potions together.

I thought for a moment and wondered what would happen if I told her the truth. How I was spending my days at the moment, capturing the strange, elusive melodies that were still appearing, almost fully formed in my imagination, and before I could stop myself, with a mixture of excitement and cheerfulness, the truth came tumbling out of my mouth.

"Yeah, I am busy as a matter of fact. I've started writing a piece of music." When I spoke the words, I became aware of a strange kind of physical tension inside, as though something felt unsettled in the air.

"Is it a pop song?" she asked in a casual tone of voice, the focus of her concentration still aimed at the drops of pale-yellow liquid she was carefully pouring from one bottle to another. "I remember you said you played in a pop band once? Or was it a punk band?"

"No, actually... it's something... classical."

You idiot. Why did you say that?

I tried to stop myself from blushing at the sheer presumptuousness of what I'd just said. Ariella was a trained classical musician, a cellist, a member of a respected orchestra, and I was nothing more than an ex-guitarist who couldn't read or write a single note of musical notation.

In the seconds of silence that followed I watched her face out of the corner of my eye to look for any hint of an expression that might suggest she thought it was a ridiculous thing for me to say too. But thankfully, nothing in her face changed and I half-wondered if she'd actually heard what I said. The physical tension that had suddenly gripped my stomach was most likely anxiety that I'd just said something stupid, I rationalized, as she continued concentrating on her task in hand. Then, out of the blue, she looked up.

"Well, if you ever finish writing it, maybe the orchestra can play it one day," she said smiling, as she handed me the bottle of this month's herbal treatment potion and gathered up the various bottles to place them back into her satchel, along with her pen and notepad.

A feeling of profound, internal release washed through me inside. It was as though a long-buried uneasiness had suddenly resolved itself, and even though the rational part of me assumed her words were just a throwaway meaningless remark said in passing, probably to be polite, in another deeper part of me, they resonated right through to the bone as I remembered Joy's message.

They are telling me that you are going to write a piece of music about your near-death experience. They say that a lot of people are going to hear it.

It suddenly seemed so obvious, so clear to me what I had to do. I had known what it felt like, to experience that other world, to be fully conscious of its beauty and unconditional love, and this music offered a way to describe it that went far beyond the limits of language or painting. It was a way of sharing everything I'd felt and experienced in that place, so that everyone would know what was waiting on the other side.

I must have been thinking this for quite a long time because I suddenly became aware that Ariella was looking at me and she had a curious expression on her face. I smiled at her in profound gratitude because, of all the things she could have said, she said the one thing that changed everything.

Without realizing it, she had pointed the way ahead.

Later on, when I thought about it some more, I realized I'd need help if I was going to pull this off. Then, the answer came and it was obvious who I should ask; there was someone right under my nose who could help. He was, in fact, the ideal person in all this.

Chapter 19

The Changeover

With a yawn that was more to do with nerves than tiredness, I sat on the sofa sipping a mug of coffee, the empty plate from my evening meal on the floor beside me, thinking about what I was going to say when he arrived. The phone conversation earlier in the week had been hard enough.

"… The thing is, I've written some music."

"And?"

"Well, it sounds a bit, er, classical."

I could hear the embarrassment in my voice as the words came out. The only saving grace was that Ian couldn't see my face.

"Classical?"

"Yeah. Classical."

That really wasn't the easiest of phone calls to make.

The television was still on in the corner of the room, but I hadn't been paying any attention to it for the past hour and the sound was turned right down. At ten to seven, I picked up the remote and switched it off. I knew he'd be on time, Ian was always punctual, so I got up from the sofa, stretched my legs to ease out the stiffness, and gathered up the empty plate and cutlery from the floor and headed into the kitchen to wash up. It was pitch black outside, raining hard and the bad weather made the portent of the evening feel even stronger.

After clearing up the dishes, I walked back over to the window to look out for his car and the same thought came to my mind, the one I'd had over and over again ever since we spoke on the phone. Would he be wondering why his dyslexic, barely literate, ex-guitarist younger brother suddenly thought he could write music that sounded 'classical'?

Ian had spent years practicing the French horn, and after graduating with his music degree, had settled down, bought a big house, started a family and got himself a successful career in engineering. I ended up at the local comprehensive, didn't pass any exams and the only musical instrument I ever learned to play was the electric guitar. And now he was coming over to my flat because I told him I'd started composing classical music and was asking for his help.

Stop worrying. Relax. It'll be fine.

Two people left the building entrance and ran across the dark car park below, got into a car and drove off, the car headlights shimmering in the puddles, and another thought surfaced as I watched them. Would he speculate that it was anything to do with my near-death experience? He'd heard the whole story from Janet when I was still in hospital, but she told me afterwards that he'd said it was most likely a hallucination, caused by the medication they gave me in the emergency department.

When I thought about it, I didn't really expect him to think anything else, Ian was always very practically-minded, but I still wondered if he'd ask me about it at some point, get my version of events at least but he hadn't, so it remained an out-of-bounds topic between the two of us, the awkward elephant in the room, the specter of the unmentioned near-death experience hanging over the silence between the polite, practical conversation that was so typical of brothers who never went near anything as dangerous as their real feelings.

At three minutes to seven, a car pulled into the car park and a lone figure got out and ran through the rain up to the warehouse entrance, disappearing from view under the flooded stone canopy. Within a few seconds, the buzzer sounded.

In the light from the hallway, Ian's coat and hair glistened with rain as I showed him in, hung up his coat and offered him a cup of tea. We hadn't seen each other in a while and as he sat in the chair at my desk by the window, smartly dressed in a dark blue suit, white shirt and plain dark blue tie, I noticed a couple of lines which had formed in between his eyebrows and I wondered if he'd been concentrating on his work for so long that they'd become permanent fixtures.

I knew he still practiced his French horn and even played in the St. Ives Chamber Orchestra with Ariella when he had time, but I got the sense his engineering job seemed to have taken over his life now.

After we'd got through the usual polite conversation, updates on his family, how well the kids were doing at school and how difficult it was these days to find parking in Wimbledon where he now lived, we finally broached the reason for his visit, the rain still pounding against the window as we talked.

"So, tell me what you need to know," he said, leaning back in the chair and shifting his weight to make himself more comfortable.

"Well... I'm writing a piece of classical music for an orchestra to play," I said, trying to sound matter-of-fact, as though this was nothing unusual.

"I see," he said, slowly. "Which orchestra?"

"The St. Ives Chamber Orchestra."

I could only imagine how this must have sounded to him, but he kept his cool and if he was curious, he didn't show it, as I told him how Ariella had suggested that the orchestra might play my piece of music if I finished composing it.

"And how are you composing this music exactly?" he asked.

"I hear the phrases of music in my head."

"Uh huh," he said slowly, obviously waiting for me to continue.

"Then I play what I hear on that synthesizer," I said, pointing to the keyboard behind him on the desk, "and record what I'm playing on Charlie's device."

"Let me get this straight. You are recording one phrase of music at a time on a voice recorder?"

"Yep."

"Then how do you know all the phrases will fit together as a larger piece of music?"

"Because in my head, they do."

His eyes drifted over to the keyboard and I thought back to the days before my accident, a parallel universe, a life left behind where Ian was the classical musician and I was the failed punk guitarist. Tonight's conversation was slightly surreal to say the least, but I knew I had to press on, tell him what I needed, get his help.

"The thing is," I continued, "some of the phrases I hear in my head have more than one instrument in them, like there's a group of musicians playing together, so I need to know what instruments make up an orchestra so that I can play each part I hear. That's what I was hoping you could help me with."

"I see," he said, looking at the synthesizer again. I noticed he was chewing his lip and his brow was furrowed. I recognized that look from old. It was his concerned expression, probably a reflection of how uncertain he was about what I was trying to pull off, using nothing other than an old plastic synthesizer, Charlie's voice recorder and a newfound belief that I could.

After a moment or two, he spoke again.

"Right, let me think of the best way to explain the makeup of a classical orchestra to you," he said as he loosened his tie, took his jacket off and placed it carefully over the back of his chair. He obviously thought it was going to be a long night...

"We can stop now if you want," he said an hour later, as I got up and wrenched open the rain-spattered window to get a breath of air.

"No, it's important," I said, as much to myself as to him. "Let me run through it one more time, to make sure I've got it straight." Repeating things back was my way of checking that I'd understood. It was one of the things Irene had suggested and it usually helped.

"So an orchestra is made up of four main groups of instruments," I said, rubbing my temples as if that would help me to remember, "strings, woodwind, brass and percussion."

"Uh huh," he prompted, waiting for me to continue.

"And in the string section, there are two groups of violins, called First Violin and Second Violin and each group can play different violin parts?"

"Uh huh."

"And the brass section typically has trombones, French horns and trumpets?"

"Uh huh."

"And the woodwind section can have flutes, oboes, clarinets, and sometimes even a bassoon?"

"Yes."

"So, basically, I need to write different parts for all the instruments in each section of the orchestra."

"That's right," he said, yawning deeply. "Look online for examples of each instrument, what their range is, how they sound. Then once you have a part in your head, just find the instrument with the sound you want and see if your synthesizer has a version of that instrument to record the part with."

Eventually, mentally exhausted, we both agreed we'd had enough for one night. With yet another huge yawn, Ian got up, pulled out his mobile phone and glanced at it, put his jacket on and headed across the room towards the hallway. Then he stopped for a moment, paused and turned back around to face me.

"Oh, there's one more thing you'll need to do."

"What's that?" I said, feeling suddenly anxious at his change of tone.

"You'll have to write the individual instrument parts down, if you want to ask an orchestra to play your music. You can't give an orchestra that," he said, pointing over to the voice recorder on the desk. "You'll need a proper score."

"A score?" I repeated.

"Yes. The musical notation written down, the sheet music telling everyone in the orchestra what to play and when to play it. It's called a score."

"I've no idea how to write music down on paper," I said, my mind suddenly paralyzed at the thought.

"Don't worry, I'll help."

"How?"

"Leave it with me. I'll think of something."

"Ian, I really appreciate all this," I said, feeling a wave of gratitude as I followed him to the door. I really did. I knew he was trying to help, and without him, I'd never manage to pull this off.

As he opened the front door, I knew there was one more thing I had to say. Before he left, I had to try to explain why I was doing it. Risk saying it out loud. I had to, after all, I needed to acknowledge the true source of my inspiration.

"The thing is," I started explaining, "I'm being guided to write this music by—"

"No," he intercut, his tone firm. "I don't think you are being guided by anything mystical. Janet told me what you believe and I'm sorry, I don't agree. I think this change in you is a result of having survived a life-threatening accident. You must have always been capable of doing something like this, maybe you've just never had the confidence before."

The tone of his voice closed down any further discussion of the subject, and with a quick awkward hug, he shut the door behind him and left. I walked back over to the window and watched as he made his way across the car park below, got into his car and weaved through the puddles out onto the road that would take him back to Wimbledon and home.

As the red taillights disappeared into the distance, I thought about the evening. There was no question he was trying to help me, I had no doubts about that at all and I felt very grateful for it. But it still hurt that he didn't believe I'd had a near-death experience and that I was being guided as a result of it. What was so difficult about accepting that?

Janet believed me. And Mum and Dad and Sarah and Joy too. None of them had questioned my version of events. In fact, until Janet told me what Ian thought about my experience, it didn't occur to me that anyone close to me would.

But as the rain splattered on the stone windowsill and I breathed in the cool night air, I realized I really wanted him to say he believed me, because this was the first time in my life I felt on track, like I'd got purpose and meaning and some deep-rooted part of me wanted his approval for the effort it had taken to achieve that.

I wanted him to see I'd changed, to acknowledge that his kid brother was making better, healthier choices now. I wanted my new life to include a new way of relating to my older brother so that the two things would come together in a satisfying, more mature whole, based on mutual respect. I wanted that so much. After all, if he refused to believe that my near-death experience was real, then how could the rest possibly fall into place, I thought, as I washed the two mugs up afterwards and headed for bed. That was the problem with being brothers. The one thing I wanted so badly from him, he could not, or would not give me.

The following Friday, yet another rainy day, a delivery van appeared, speeding into the car park below, a spray of rain whipping off its wheels as it ploughed through the deep puddles. After coming to an abrupt halt, the driver got out, opened the back doors of the van, disappeared inside for a few seconds, then emerged carrying a large and seemingly heavy cardboard box which he carried with some difficulty to the main building doorway. A few seconds later, my door buzzer sounded and a voice boomed out of the small intercom speaker.

"Parcel delivery for Daveed Dutch-feld," said a heavily

accented voice, clearly someone on a tight deadline.

"Hold on, I'll be right down," I said, hurrying to put on my shoes.

The large box was heavy and the driver said he still had fifty deliveries to drop off before the end of his shift, so was in far too much of a rush to help me carry it upstairs, which meant by the time I had half-carried, half-dragged the box up the two flights and maneuvered it through my flat doorway to place it down on the floor of my sitting room, the pain in my left arm was excruciating and I was sweating at the sheer effort it had taken. I'd had to stop on the stairwell several times on the way up, gritting my teeth to cope with the pain.

Once I'd recovered enough to ignore the deep throb inside the remaining muscle and bone of my left arm, I began to cut at the tape around the box with a pair of scissors, and when I turned the box around, I recognized the return address in Wimbledon, written in felt tip on the side panel. Then I opened the two flaps of the lid and couldn't believe what I was looking at…

"Ian?"

"Yes?" said the voice on the other end of the phone.

"Thank you," I said, holding my mobile phone in one hand as I stared at the Power Mac G4 computer, monitor and keyboard emerging from a bed of discarded bubble wrap and torn cardboard. "Where did it come from?"

"I bought it a couple of years ago to do some engineering designs at home, but I've got a laptop now. You can have it on long-term loan."

"I don't know what to say…"

"There's a lead in the box. It will connect your synthesizer to the Mac," he said with a tone of voice that suggested I should understand exactly why this would be useful.

"Thanks. But why would I connect them?"

"Because I've also loaded Finale PrintMusic on the Mac. It's a computer software program that automatically transcribes anything played on a keyboard and converts it into a musical score, if the keyboard is plugged into the computer."

"You mean it automatically writes music down, like on paper?" I said, not quite sure of what I was hearing, but suddenly alert to the possibility of hope that this software might offer.

"Yep. It will produce a proper orchestral score for each instrumental part that you play on the synthesizer, and you can print the score out too, if that's what you want to do."

"Wow... yeah... thanks... I don't know what to say..."

As he carried on explaining how it worked, I felt an incredible sense of relief and gratitude and a strange lump in my throat, though I had no idea why I should feel so sad at the same time as feeling incredibly touched at his gesture.

This strangely sentimental yet happy mood continued as I assembled the components and found myself, two hours later, with the Power Mac up and running on my desk, Finale Press software blinking ready on the large, inviting computer screen and the instruction manual open at the first page.

Chapter 20

This Means Something

As I sat down at my desk with a steaming hot mug of coffee, it was still early. Sunlight was streaming in through the living room windows and the sky was a cheery bright blue. Stretching my legs, I leaned back in my chair and made myself comfortable as I clicked on the Play button in the Finale Press program and listened to the two distinct pieces of music coming out of the small speaker attached to the computer. It was a last listen-through before I e-mailed the audio files to Ian.

The first piece of music was meant to sound very peaceful and calm, because that was how I felt when I found myself in the world of Light. From the opening notes to when the last strings died away, I hoped it would transport the listener to that beautiful, peaceful world.

The second piece continued to describe my experience of being in that otherworldly place, what it felt like to be unconditionally loved, with no sense of fear, no questioning, only acceptance and trust of the compassionate energy that surrounded me as a voice inside my head whispered, *You are safe, everything is well. You are loved.*

As I clicked on the send button and the e-mail left my inbox carrying its two music file attachments, I felt a strange sense of calm at the thought that someone else in the world would listen to my music for the very first time, a calmness that lasted for the next few days as I waited for his response...

"Hello?" I said, feeling my stomach grip as I recognized the caller's number.

"Hi, it's me, Ian."

"Oh. Hi," I replied, suddenly feeling acutely anxious.

"I've listened to your music."

"And...?" In the space between moments as I waited for his response, I felt the bottom drop out of my stomach as though I'd just stepped over the edge of a cliff.

"It's—"

At that precise moment, the signal on my mobile seemed to drop for a second and I couldn't make out what he said. Or maybe I froze in fear of hearing something negative. I couldn't tell which. All I know is that the conversation suddenly disappeared for a few seconds.

When I thought back afterwards, I was sure he said the word, "good", but I couldn't be certain and I couldn't bring myself to interrupt, ask him to repeat what he said, especially as he started talking about some small detail in one of the instrumental parts. I wanted him to say what he thought of it again, clearer, more slowly. I wanted him to say he was impressed, so I could pause, take stock and really feel the impact of his approval inside, so I could truly believe that he thought my music was good; in fact, not just good, but good enough.

Instead, my mind hooked onto one thought and wouldn't let go, and the long-ingrained habit of self-doubt made me question what I heard, chipping away at the meaning behind it so that the word I thought I heard was drowned out in a louder internal voice that crowed, *Maybe he did say good, but it's still not good enough.*

With an effort, I made myself refocus on the conversation, just as Ian started talking about the overall structure of the two pieces.

"So, in the first and second movement of a symphony, there should be a change in tone between the two pieces."

"A symphony? What's that?" I said, trying to catch up in the conversation.

He sighed, and even though I couldn't see him, I could imagine his mind working, trying to think of the easiest way to explain yet another thing to his woefully undereducated younger brother.

"Okay," he said in his slightly slower explaining tone of voice. "Classical music consists of a number of different styles. The most popular styles are the opera, concerto, and symphony. You're definitely not writing an opera, so forget that one. A concerto usually has a solo instrument throughout, with the orchestra providing the accompaniment. As you don't have a solo instrument, you are not writing a concerto either. What I think you are composing is a symphony, because in your two pieces, you've got the beginnings of an extended piece of music. Symphonies typically have three or sometimes four movements. Think of these as chapters in a book, each one unique, with its own mood and tone, but also part of something larger. That's what I think you've composed here, the first two movements of a symphony. That's what I heard when I listened to the two files."

"Really? A symphony?" I repeated, incredulously.

"That's what it sounds like to me. And now you've passed the halfway mark, you should print out the score of what you've composed so far and show it to Ariella to get her feedback. After all, you said it was her suggestion that inspired you to do this."

Two days later, I found myself outside the Archers Arms, a bar in St. Ives that Ariella had suggested meeting in. The familiar smell of beer and wine wafted through the air as I pulled open the heavy wooden door and entered, two printed scores carried under my arm. The bright sunshine streamed in through the bar windows and its rays were filled with tiny floating particles as the light settled on the thick varnish covering the dark-brown furniture.

I had to blink a couple of times as the contrast between the bright daylight outside and the gloomy interior took some getting used to. I could smell old beer too, which I guessed was coming from the heavily-stained carpet.

As my eyes adjusted, I could make out the layout of the bar.

A few round tables and chairs, a couple of bench seats along the wall and a long bar, behind which stood an overweight bald bartender, sweating and red-faced as he pumped out a pint of beer from one of the beer taps.

I heard him tell the customer at the bar that he'd have to change the barrel and he disappeared off through a door at the back of the bar, so I sat down at an empty table. At the next table, a young couple sat, looking at their mobile phones, and on the other side of the bar, three older men were talking loudly about football as they drank their pints.

After a few minutes, the bartender reappeared behind the bar and tried the beer pump again. At first, the pump produced a stuttering, gassy-looking froth, but then clear dark brown liquid started flowing smoothly into the clean pint glass he was holding under the tap.

"That's better," he said, holding the glass up to the sunlight and peering closely at the velvet-brown liquid still swirling around as the bubbles floated upwards. After a few seconds, a thin white head of foam slowly formed on top of the pint. Beads of sweat glistened on the bartender's red forehead. It was obviously warm work changing the barrel. When the glass was full, he carefully placed the pint of beer down in front of the customer stood at the bar.

"Looks good," said the man, handing over a handful of change. I thought so too; from where I was sat, it looked like a perfect pint.

It really was amazing, when you thought about it. Just four basic ingredients, barley, hops, yeast and water. That was all it took for the alchemy to happen. Just extract the sugar from the barley, use the yeast to turn it into alcohol and carbon dioxide, and hey presto, you had beer.

Then I wondered, how did someone think of putting these four things together to invent alcohol 5000 years ago? Maybe they were trying to make the first-ever loaf of bread and somehow ended up with a clay pot of strangely intoxicating, amber-colored liquid instead. What a discovery. Second only to the invention of the wheel in terms of direct impact on humanity, although arguably nowhere near as useful.

The bartender looked over at me expectantly, but I'd already decided I'd order my drink when the girls got here. I was early, but it didn't matter. I'd wait.

I looked around at the other customers, then picked up a beer mat and started to read the small lettering on the back until the outline of two figures suddenly appeared in front of me, silhouetted against the bright shaft of sunlight streaming in through the nearest window. It was Ariella and her friend, Gillian, who also played cello in the same orchestra.

"Hi. Thanks for coming. What would you like to drink?" I asked each in turn, pulling out an empty stool next to the bench seat and moving my bag onto the floor so that they could both sit down.

"I'll have a white wine spritzer, please," said Ariella.

"That sounds good, I'll have the same," said Gillian. "Thanks."

A warning bell went off in my head as I stood in front of the bar and the sweaty barman glanced over in my direction again. But I remembered exactly what to do. I took a deep breath as the bartender came up to serve me and I heard myself say the words, loud and clear.

"Two white wine spritzers, and a Diet Coke and lemon, please."

"Does the lady want ice and lemon in her Coke?" he asked, looking over at the girls.

"The Coke is for me and no ice, thanks."

"Not drinking today?" he asked, blandly. But his tone had a kind of professional, casual curiosity to it that meant he wasn't really interested in my answer. But I didn't care if he wasn't interested.

"No, I don't drink alcohol," I said, clearly and firmly. I had to be clear. As Irene said, agreeing to meet someone at a bar would always be hard for someone like me. But so long as I accepted the bad feelings, knowing that they'd eventually pass, I would manage to do it. I would manage to stay sober. One day at a time.

When I returned to the table, Ariella and Gillian were already leafing through the pages of the score. Ariella's facial expression was difficult to read, and it was hard to know where to look or what to do as she silently turned over page after page of the neatly printed score, as though she was speed-reading a large book. Gillian's eyes moved just as quickly over the pages in her copy too. I still hadn't got a clue how to read any of the strange dots and lines that appeared on the paper when I printed out the scores on Janet and Charlie's printer.

The silence was almost unbearable. I wondered if the music was so bad, that they were playing for time, trying to figure out how to pass comment on the score without offending me. Still more minutes passed as they turned page after page, and I glanced at them both as they continued to silently read the score. Now, I could swear Ariella's expression looked like she was puzzled about something and I didn't know what to make of it. Then, as she turned the last page and closed the score, she shook her head slightly, her eyes wide and curious.

"This is good, really good," she said, an unmistakable tone of surprise in her voice. "You never told me you knew how to compose music like this."

I smiled broadly, relieved at her response.

"And how did you produce such a professional-looking orchestral score?" she asked, her fingers running slowly over the cover page. I got the impression she was making sure it really existed.

"I didn't," I replied. "I mean, I composed all of the music using a synthesizer, but I can't read or write musical notation at all. My brother Ian sorted me out with a computer which connected to the keyboard, then I played all the individual parts and the computer program turned it into sheet music, and then I printed out the finished score."

I said this as though it were the most natural thing in the world, but she stared at me in a way I'd never seen her do before. Then Gillian spoke, but not to me, more to Ariella.

"It is really good, isn't it," she said, but it didn't sound like a question. "We should do it."

Ariella nodded, then turned to me and, for the second time in our friendship, said something I wasn't expecting.

"We think you should show it to Chris, the orchestra conductor. Tell him we think the orchestra would like to perform it when you've finished it," she said as she rummaged around in her bag, pulled out her mobile phone and began tapping on the screen. "I'll text you his number so you can contact him."

For a moment, I wondered if I'd misheard her, but when she kept smiling at me and the incoming text message alert rang out on my phone, I figured I hadn't.

"I will. Thanks. Really. Thanks," I said, trying not to sound too relieved. I didn't want to come across like I expected them to reject it, even if I secretly did. But they really seemed to like what they'd seen, and somewhere deep inside, I felt like something important had just happened.

Then they both smiled so genuinely that an unexpected sense of happiness rushed through me.

"What's it called?" asked Ariella.

The Divine Light," I said, a big grin forming on my face.

The following Monday morning, I found myself standing outside the grand Victorian detached town house that belonged to Chris, the St. Ives Chamber Orchestra's resident conductor. I walked up the gravel path to the imposing front door and rang the doorbell. Its chimes echoed inside the large old house for what seemed like ages.

As I waited, I checked the carrier bag one more time, to make sure it contained *The Divine Light*, Movements One and Two score, safe in its plastic cover.

I had no idea what I was supposed to say to Chris at the meeting, but Ian had said it was okay to show him what I'd done up to date, even if the symphony was still unfinished. Apparently, orchestras decide what to perform many months in advance of a concert, so if Chris liked it, I'd still have plenty of time to finish off the third and final movement. That was what Ian said anyway and I trusted him.

Someone turned a big latch inside and the heavy door swung open. As my eyes adjusted to the dark hallway, I saw a middle-aged man stood in the open doorway, wearing brown corduroy trousers, a dark blue polo neck jumper and brown brogues. His glasses sat halfway down his nose and his hair was thick, dark blond and wavy, and he looked just like I'd imagined.

"Ah, hello. You must be David. We spoke on the phone. Come in, come in," he said in a friendly tone of voice.

I stepped into the hallway, shut the door behind me, wiped my shoes carefully on the thick rush doormat and followed him into the house. He led me into a large room, furnished with antiques, bookcases stuffed full of books and a grand piano, then disappeared off to make tea for us both. As I was alone in the room, I had a closer look at the piano. It was lovely. Old warm spruce wood casing with a decorative inlay of what looked like maple.

Nice inlay work, I thought to myself and I was sorely tempted to press one of the ebony black and slightly yellowed keys to hear what the piano sounded like, but decided against it, the silence hung too heavily to break with my clumsy one-handed playing.

Chris returned with a small tray in his hands and placed it on the table between two old, comfortable sofas. I sat on the sofa on one side of the table and Chris sat down on the opposite side. I tried not to spill my tea out of the delicate china cup and saucer he'd given me as I explained to him that I'd written two movements of a symphony, and Ariella and Gillian had suggested that I show them to him.

Part of me had imagined that he might be surprised that someone like me would attempt to write a symphony, but his expression didn't give anything away and he carried on sipping his tea.

I didn't know what to say next, so I handed him the score and he put his cup and saucer down on the table, sat back and made himself comfortable, then opened it to the first page. A clock ticked loudly and the sound of it echoed round the house as I watched his eyes move across each page in turn as though he was skim-reading the pages of a book. Several more minutes passed in silence before he eventually got to the last page of the second movement, closed the score and handed it back to me.

"Yes, the girls are right. This is good," he said. "We have a concert scheduled to take place in July next year and we could include *The Divine Light* if you complete it by then."

That was all he said. As easy as that. He didn't say much more, just a rough timescale of when he'd need the full scores by and how the orchestra usually rehearsed in the week before the concert. But I wasn't really listening, because I was still reeling from the fact that the orchestra would be performing it in July. Then he showed me out, and with a thud, the big front door closed and that was it; the meeting was over and as I walked along the road, I wondered if I'd just imagined the entire conversation.

July. He said July, definitely. I was sure he did. July next year. That gave me seven months in which to finish off the whole symphony, plus have the entire printed score available for the orchestra to rehearse before the concert date. That thought made the pit of my stomach drop, so I put it to the back of my mind and decided to just concentrate on finishing the symphony. Nothing more than that. No big game plan, no end game.

Just finish it.

Chapter 21

Halley's Comet

There were only ten weeks left before the concert and the thought of it weighed in and out of my dreams, sometimes positive, sometimes with a feeling of dread at the thought of not completing everything in time.

Last night's dream was one of the bad ones. Vague images from the dream lingered as I woke up, flashes of me running to get to the concert venue, not being allowed in, struggling to persuade the person on the door that I was, in fact, the composer and I was needed inside, but not being allowed to enter.

I opened my eyes. It looked sunny outside; I could tell by the quality of bright, early spring light coming in through the bedroom window. My first thought was that I needed a pee, but I still wasn't fully awake yet, so I closed my eyes again to allow myself the luxury of slipping back into a world of half-sleep until my mobile phone started ringing and forced me to open my eyes again.

"Hi, mate."

"Jimmy, hi, one second, let me get up," I replied, holding the mobile phone in one hand as I managed to maneuver myself to sit upright on the edge of the bed before continuing the conversation. "How's it going? You and Matt still working at the Cambridge site?"

"Nah," he replied, "finished that couple of weeks ago. Working on a site near Heathrow Airport now."

I could hear the sound of heavy machinery and men's voices in the background.

"You at work now?" I asked, feeling slightly guilty that I had only just woken up.

"Yeah, just on me tea break. So, how's things then?"

"Good," I said, stifling a yawn. "Got the concert premiere coming up soon so working my backside off to get everything finished."

"Jeez. It's bloody nuts. You a classical composer. Still can't get me head round the idea."

"You are still coming to the concert, aren't you?" I said, now making my way towards the bathroom. "I'll put your names on the door."

"Wouldn't miss it for the world. Anyway, listen, got something to tell you."

"What?"

"Guess who I ran into last week?"

"Who?"

"Anna, at a party in Hoxton."

"Really?" I said, coming to an abrupt halt in the hallway, before heading into the sitting room where the mobile reception was usually better. "How is she?"

"Good. Asked after you."

"Did she?" I said, trying not to sound too interested.

"Yeah."

"Was she with anyone?" I asked, half-afraid to hear the answer.

"Oh, some girlfriend, from work I think. I got introduced but couldn't remember her name."

"So, she wasn't with her boyfriend then?"

"Nah, apparently they're not going out anymore."

"Says who?"

"Says Anna. He got transferred to Edinburgh, something to do with his job. He asked her to go with him, but she didn't want to."

"How did she seem?" I asked, doing my best to sound casual, mildly interested at best. "Was she upset about it?"

"She didn't look too upset to me," he replied. "Oh, she said to tell you good luck for the concert as well."

"How does she know about that?"

"Because I told her about it, Mozart."

"Did she seem... was she..." By now, I was aware of a tight knot in my stomach.

"She was blown away, mate. That's what I'm calling about, thought you might like to know."

"Thanks, Jimmy, really appreciate it."

"So, are you gonna phone her then?"

As he said this, I felt an overwhelming, crazy urge to finish the call as quickly as possible and dial Anna's number immediately, to talk to her, arrange to meet up, tell her how sorry I was at not asking her out before, acknowledge how stupid I'd been and explain how, with Irene's help, I was working through things, doing my best to understand why I was still so afraid of starting a relationship with her...

"You still there?" asked Jimmy after a few moments' silence.

"Yeah, sorry, lost the phone signal," I lied, stuck between wanting to ask his advice on what to say to her and a deeper, older ingrained habit of keeping things to myself, not wanting anyone's sympathy or even worse, pity, and I heard myself clumsily changing the subject instead.

"What are you doing at the weekend, anything exciting?"

"Going to a party in Shoreditch. You wanna come?" he said, cheerfully.

"Love to, but I can't."

"Why not?"

"I'm off to Heacham today."

"Where the hell is that?"

"On the Norfolk Coast. My sister has rented a holiday cottage and I'm invited for the weekend."

"You'll need a passport and jabs that far outside London."

"Funny as ever," I retorted, trying to sound upbeat as we said our goodbyes and arranged to speak the following week, but after the call ended, I sat staring at the phone as the crazy, urgent need to speak to Anna subsided and a wave of self-doubt took its place.

Don't phone, just concentrate on your work, it's safer that way.

Irene was right, the fear of trying to have a relationship felt stronger than the fear of not having one and I had no idea why.

By now, it had started raining outside, and as the drops hammered against the window, I looked across at the clock and realized it was after 9am. Once I'd showered and made myself a strong cup of coffee, it didn't take me long to pack an overnight bag for the Heacham trip, just one change of clothes, jeans, a T-shirt and jumper, shaving kit and a notepad and pen, which were small enough to fit into the inside pocket of my jacket. By the time I'd found my watch and had two pieces of toast, I was finally ready to leave the flat and put Jimmy's phone conversation to the back of my mind.

Janet said a couple of days by the sea would do me good as weekdays and weekends had become one long blur lately as I made the last push to finish off the symphony. But I wasn't going for a holiday, there was still more work to do, and at some point, a vague idea had formed that if I went away, had a break from the flat, the change of scene might give me inspiration to write the lyrics for the new vocal part I'd composed in the final movement.

Recently, I'd heard a melody in my head that I knew instinctively was for voice. The idea of having to put lyrics together for a classical singer filled me with a sense of dread. I couldn't write a legible shopping list, let alone poetical lyrics, but until I had the words for the vocal part, I couldn't approach any singers to ask if they'd perform at the concert. At least Heacham would be somewhere unfamiliar, and maybe the unfamiliar would help the words to come. That was my idea anyway.

Janet had given me directions to the cottage. I was to get the train to Cambridge and King's Lynn, then the bus to Heacham where Charlie would meet me. She kept asking me if I'd be okay, going back to Huntingdon station and travelling on a train again, but I reassured her that I'd talked it over with Irene and had even been back to stand on the platform as part of my recovery therapy.

Despite this, I knew I'd find it hard on the day, and sure enough, as the Cambridge-bound train approached the Huntingdon station platform, my heart started pounding as I carefully avoided looking at the gap between the train and the platform, and it wasn't until I'd boarded the train and sat down in the nearest empty seat that my heart slowed down and my breathing relaxed again. To distract myself, I picked up a newspaper someone had left on the empty seat opposite and an article on one of the grubby, well-read pages caught my attention.

Eta Aquariids Meteor Shower – where stargazers can see it

The Eta Aquariids meteor shower will peak tonight, between 3–5am. The meteor shower occurs when the earth passes through the dust and debris of Halley's Comet, which orbits the sun every 75 years. As the dust and debris hit the Earth's atmosphere, the particles burn up and appear to the naked eye as streaks of light in the night sky. Stargazers will find it more difficult to see the meteors this year as tonight's peak night coincides with a full moon. However, if you are lucky enough to see it, you can expect to see up to 20 meteors per hour, with occasional bursts of over 100 per hour.

The Heacham beach house Janet and Charlie had rented was lovely, with white wooden paneled walls and old floorboards in all the rooms. The back of the house had a sun room, blue wooden paneled walls and long windows running along the length of it, with a door that led straight out to a tiny patch of garden, which had an old wooden gate at the end.

Literally right outside the gate were rolling sand dunes, perfect golden sand covered in wild tufts of beach grass, or Marram grass as Janet named it. It was a really lovely location, and Janet and the boys were really excited as they showed me around.

After a long beach walk, Charlie organized everyone in the kitchen, and an hour later, dinner was served and we all sat in front of the little television in the corner of the sitting room for the rest of the evening, until one by one, we all drifted off to bed.

The window in my first-floor bedroom looked out across the top of the sand dunes and to the sea beyond. Even though it had been a lovely evening, as I lay in bed in the dark, listening to the distant crash of waves on the shore, the constant worry about not having written any lyrics preyed on my mind.

Janet and Charlie had been really welcoming, but I felt torn, unsure that anything useful would come of this trip and half-regretted leaving my flat, where at least I had everything I needed to work if any inspiration came. But once I'd got myself comfortable in the strange bed, tiredness began to catch up with me and I eventually settled into a restless sleep.

It felt like I'd been asleep for a few hours when something woke me up. I had no idea of the time, but guessed it was probably well after midnight. It looked really dark outside and I could just make out a sliver of moonlight coming in through the top corner of the window, far too beautiful to ignore.

Sitting up, I reached across and opened the little window to look outside and the fresh, salty air smelled good. As my eyes adjusted to the darkness, the black silhouette of the top of the sand dunes came into focus and the distinct loud roar of crashing waves of the incoming tide seemed to get louder with each wave as the brilliant moonlight reflected back off the white crests of foaming wave water.

An instinct inside me said, "Get up." So I did. I put on my jeans, T-shirt and a jumper, opened the bedroom door as quietly as I could, and tiptoed down the creaky, wooden stairs in my socks, carrying my shoes in my hand. The sitting room was in darkness except for the grey luminous moonlight coming in through the window and reflecting off the white wooden paneling. The clock on the wall said 3am.

Another instinct inside me said, "Go outside," so I put on my shoes and jacket, and as quietly as I could, opened the back door of the sun lounge and went outside into the back garden and shut the door, leaving the latch up so that I could get back in again.

"Go to the beach," my instinct said, so I crossed the tiny back garden, out through the gate and up along the path across the little sand dunes dotted with dense, grey-green tufts of Marram grass. Under the starry sky and brilliant full moonlight, the beach was almost uniformly luminous grey, a strange alien landscape, but still beautiful. I sat at the edge of the nearest sand dune, and even though it was the early hours of the morning, the sand felt warm and soft.

Under this jeweled canopy, I laid back and looked up at the stars above, the sound of the rhythmic waves pulling my breathing into the same, relaxed, slow rhythm as the sea. Lying there, I could have been the only person in the world.

Thousands of grains of warm sand slipped through my fingers, and it felt cool to the touch. I looked at the tiny glittering grains of sand still sat in the palm of my cupped hand as they reflected the moonlight, then turned my head back towards the night sky. It looked beautiful overhead, a million stars twinkled to the sound of the nearby crashing waves and a big, bold moon lit up the northernmost part of the sky, just above the horizon.

Then I saw them directly overhead. Exploding streaks of light crossing the sky. Just two at first. Then, more. Three, four, maybe ten. Then lots, like fireworks going off, brilliant points of light streaking from north to south, fading as fast as they appeared, and I felt like I was the only human being on the planet watching them and it felt magical.

It must have been just before five when I reached inside my jacket and felt around for the notepad and pen. And as the meteors became harder to see against the faint velvet-pink and purple tones of the slowly lightening sky, and the setting moon began to dissolve as the first rays of sunlight appeared above the horizon, for a moment, I was back into the world of Light, just as I remembered it and the words came to me like leaves falling from a great tree, and in the quiet stillness of the dawn, I wrote them down in wonder.

"Hello. Is that Julian?"

"Yes?" said a well-spoken, soft voice.

"Ariella from the St. Ives Orchestra gave me your number. She said you're the lead tenor singer in the St Ives Choral Society group." I had no idea what a Choral Society group was, but Ariella had assured me that Julian was "the best" as she put it, and in fact, I would be very lucky to get him.

"Yes, that's right," the voice said cautiously, clearly waiting for me to explain who I was and the reason for my call.

Once I'd explained, he invited me over to his house to talk. I took the score round and the lyrics to the third movement, and just like the others, he read each page of the score like it was a book, turning page after page in complete silence. What must it be like, I wondered, to be able to read music like that? As though you could hear it in your head by making sense of all the dots and lines on the page.

Julian got to the last page, then closed the score and handed it back to me.

"Do you have the lyrics?"

I handed him the piece of paper I had written them on.

"Give me a moment," he said, and he walked over to the window and read the words.

And so my soul sings
My body broken, yet feels no pain
Light of all, you embrace me
And so my soul sings
Of hands lay on me
The love of light you surround me
Sea of stars shine for me
You've shown me infinity
The pure and divine Light
That moment of your love remains
As savior, life creator
The Divine Light

He stayed silent for what seemed like ages, then looked up again.

"Who wrote these words?"

"I did."

"And the music?"

"Yeah. I did that too."

"And the concert is when?"

"Saturday 12th July."

"Okay. I'll do it."

Just like that. Just a friendly squeeze of my hand as we shook hands to say goodbye and that was that. *The Divine Light* had its tenor singer.

The third movement had its words and someone to sing them, and my symphony was now complete. All I could do now was to wait for the first orchestral rehearsal scheduled to take place just before the concert. There was nothing else I could do in the meantime. My part in this was done.

Chapter 22

Posh Orchestras, Do's and Don'ts

The date was clearly marked in the calendar hanging on my kitchen wall. Admittedly, it looked a bit childish, but I'd drawn a big red circle around today's date, June 30th, as it marked the first of the two orchestra rehearsals, both scheduled to take place in the week before the July concert. This was the moment when I'd hear *The Divine Light* played out loud by a proper orchestra for the first time ever.

A growing sense of nerves was driving me to make sure I was prepared for this evening even though I had no idea what else I could do. I'd never had anything to do with classical musicians before and the thought of how much my life had changed to this point, how unlikely it was that someone like me would end up composing a classical symphony made me feel slightly sick at the thought of what lay ahead.

The sun was warm on my back as I sat down at my desk, finishing off my toast and coffee as I looked at the River Great Ouse outside, going through my mental list one more time to make sure nothing had been forgotten.

Fifty individual orchestral scores printed and delivered to Ian's house. Check. As I mentally ticked this off on my imaginary list, I nodded, as if to convince myself of the fact that the musicians' scores had all been printed out on A4-sized music notation paper and bound together as fifty separate, complete scores, a specific, dedicated one for each of the orchestra musicians. A full A3-sized Conductor's score had also been printed for Chris, and they had all been delivered by the print shop manager to Ian's Wimbledon home, ready to be transported to tonight's rehearsal in Ian's car.

The print shop had been helpful, especially when Ian phoned

them to explain exactly how the sheet music should be printed after I was unable to answer even their most basic of questions about the musical scores that I'd just e-mailed them. That was embarrassing to say the least.

Ian had already explained to me how the classical music world worked, and it was clear that orchestras operated in a different universe to the one I'd known playing in bands. Pop musicians typically rehearsed for ages before playing a gig, memorizing songs by repeated playing.

In complete contrast, classical musicians were trained to read a new score by sight rather than learning a piece by rote, which meant concert pieces were usually only rehearsed one or two times even if the music was unfamiliar or new, typically in the same week as the concert itself. Not what I was expecting, but as he pointed out with a serious tone to his voice, orchestral musicians didn't start practicing one week before a concert, it was more like several years before, because it took a long time to learn how to sight-read that well.

Next on my imaginary list was going through the route to the rehearsal hall in my head once more, to make sure I'd arrive on time. Chris the conductor had phoned me earlier in the week with instructions, although I had to admit, as soon as I heard his voice, I tensed up with nerves. He gave me the date and venue for the first rehearsal and said to arrive at 8.45pm. He said they'd be rehearsing another symphony for the first hour, then they'd concentrate on *The Divine Light* symphony for the rest of the evening.

Since then, I'd thought everything through very carefully, calculating exactly how much time it would take me to get to the rehearsal hall as I didn't want to turn up too early. That would look too keen and amateurish, and it would be obvious that I didn't know the ropes and would end up getting in people's way. No, I'd decided I'd arrive at the rehearsal hall with all the scores at 8.45pm precisely, just as Chris had said. That was the proper way of doing it, the insider's way.

Small, nagging doubts kept coming into my mind for the rest of the day as I became increasingly anxious at the thought there was some vital, key detail that I had not taken into account. At six o'clock, I changed my shirt for the third time and looked at myself in the mirror again and sighed.

"Get a grip," I told myself. "You look fine." Then I changed my shirt again.

At 7pm, I tried to watch some television, but couldn't concentrate, so I tried to eat something, but my stomach felt unsettled, so I ended up leaving most of the food on the plate. I didn't feel that hungry anyway.

Finally, after restlessly channel-hopping for half an hour, at last it was time to go. Putting on my jacket, I checked myself in the mirror one last time, grabbed my keys, wallet, notepad and pen, left the flat and crossed the road to wait at the empty bus stop opposite.

Within a few minutes, right on schedule, the brightly-lit, half-empty bus pulled up at the stop and I sat down in one of the front seats for the short journey into St. Ives, looking out of the window as the bus crossed the River Great Ouse over the 15th century bridge, rumbled on past the old St. Ledger's Chapel, then along Bridge Street, past the old Jacobean houses that lined either side, before finally stopping in Market Hill square.

From there, it was just a short walk down Crown Street, past the Free Church building and then first left onto the small backstreet where the rehearsal hall was located. The hall was a former Victorian warehouse, set back from the road by a red-brick wall, which marked out the dimly-lit grounds of its own small car park, now full of cars.

A lone figure was waiting under the unlit stone canopy of the doorway, and as I got closer, I realized it was Ian.

"You're late," he said, tight-lipped and unsmiling as I walked up the three stone steps to the doorway.

"I'm not, Chris said 8.45pm," but Ian cut in before I could finish what I was saying.

"We have to go in right now. One thing you don't do is to keep an orchestra waiting," he said, flashing me a critical stare. As I followed him in, the anxiety that had been building inside me all day turned into a stab of panic as I suddenly questioned the reliability of my memory of the conversation with Chris about tonight's arrangements.

Ian led me into a rather drab lobby with dark wooden paneling along the walls and a small wooden table, on which a large pile of thick musical scores were neatly stacked. A vague, musty damp smell hit my nostrils as I entered the building.

He picked up the scores and headed towards a door at the far end of the lobby. I pulled the heavy door open for him and followed inside, then the door swung back and hit the wooden surround with a loud bang as I let go of it. The quiet chattering sound we'd walked in on stopped in an instant, and fifty pairs of eyes turned to stare at the source of the loud noise.

The rehearsal room reminded me of the Spiritualist Church, an old municipal building with worn floorboards, faded magnolia-painted walls and windows set high in the wall. In this large, high-ceilinged room, the orchestra musicians were sat in sweeping semicircles of old wooden chairs, three rows deep and were all now looking at me over the tops of their music stands.

Unsure what to do, I looked round for Ian. He had already walked across the room and placed the pile of scores on a table at the back of the hall. In pin-drop silence, I walked across the hall to join him, and with each step, it felt like the fifty pairs of eyes were following me like laser beam searchlights.

"I'm sorry if I'm late," I said out loud, not quite sure who I was addressing but aware that I seemed to have made some monumental error in timing. I was secretly hoping someone might say, "Don't worry, it's okay," but no one did.

Chris looked up from a score he was studying on his

conductor's stand, and in a slightly distracted voice said, "Ah, hello, yes, okay. Just wait over there, we will be doing your piece in a few minutes," his baton pointing towards Ian's direction.

I realized I must have made a mistake with the timing, or perhaps somewhere along the line, the rehearsal time had changed, and because my presence wasn't important or maybe not even wanted, they had forgotten to tell me. Whatever it was, this wasn't the first impression I was hoping to make.

Chris raised his baton, tapped on his conductor's stand and the fifty pairs of eyes turned from me to him.

"Let's take it from bar 165 to the end, shall we?" he said, raising his arms. Then, as he swept his baton up in the air, the entire orchestra of fifty individuals suddenly became as one, bows flying across the necks of violins and cellos in synchronized gliding movements, wind instruments raised up to mouths and blown in unison and every instrument guided by the constant up and down movements of the small baton stick.

I listened to the music they played and instantly compared it to my piece. Was my symphony like this? Of this standard? Did my music sound 'classical' enough, whatever that was? My heart was racing by now and I could feel small beads of sweat on my forehead.

After a few minutes of playing, the kettle drums boomed, and with a loud climactic chord, the piece came to an end. Almost immediately, the sound of muted chatter rose up from the orchestra as the musicians folded up the scores on their music stands, as though they were closing a book they'd finished reading, and then suddenly, without warning, Chris looked up and made an announcement that cut across the quiet backdrop of conversation in the room.

"Right, everyone. As you know, we are going to be performing a new piece at next week's concert. It's a symphony, composed by David Ditchfield, who is here with us this evening. The piece is called *The Divine Light* and tonight we will be rehearsing all three movements."

Then he looked over at me and said loudly across the room, "David, have you got the scores for everyone please?"

Fifty heads spun round in unison, and under the silent gaze of the entire orchestra, I found myself rooted to the spot, unable to respond to his request. There seemed to be a slightly charged atmosphere in the room as I turned around and stared blankly at the pile of scores, paralyzed, clearly revealing the fact I had no idea which copy was for which musician. All I knew was that there were different scores for different instruments in the pile, but beyond that, nothing.

For a moment, I froze inside, horrified that the truth had now been so publicly revealed, and then I started imagining they were all looking at me thinking, "Does he even know what he's doing?"

Thankfully, Ian immediately picked up the pile of scores and began distributing them with the assured expert air of someone who knew an orchestra layout well and knew exactly where everyone was placed in that orchestra.

Chris was handed his larger conductor's score which he opened at the first page, and I watched him smooth the binding crease so that it lay flat on his music stand. Eventually, Ian reached the far side of the room, and everyone had a copy of the score. Chris then lifted his head and looked over in my direction and said the very thing I'd been dreading ever since I arrived in the hall.

"David. Would you like to say a few words to the orchestra before we begin?"

My heart started pounding as the fifty pairs of eyes continued their laser beam scrutiny as I walked up to the front of the orchestra and stood next to Chris at the conductor's music stand. My arms suddenly felt like they didn't belong to me and I didn't know what to do with them, so I put my hands in my jacket pocket, and I cleared my throat and tried to calm the feeling of panic in my mind as I reached for the right words.

"Hm. Hello... (silence)... um... I wrote this symphony after having an accident... (silence)... huh, hm... the thing is... I fell under the wheels of a train. Then, in the emergency department of the hospital, something happened. Something I can't explain..."

As soon as I started talking about my near-death experience, the truth and conviction of my story steadied my voice. This was the first time I'd talked about it to such a large group of people. Obviously, I edited out the part about being guided from spirit to help compose *The Divine Light*. No way was I going to mention it here. I'd learned my lesson from Ian's reaction, but I told them everything else, and as I spoke, I could feel the intensity of a group of people listening to every word I said, and for a few short moments, I felt everything was going to be okay. But that feeling didn't last for long.

After I'd finished speaking, I thought I saw a couple of people nod with approval, but most of the musicians remained inscrutable, their faces betraying no emotion that I could recognize. Then, as though by some secret agreement, everyone silently opened the score and placed it on their music stands and raised up their instruments ready as Chris raised his conductor's baton in the air.

Unsure what to do, I stayed at the front. I wasn't sure if I was supposed to, but no one told me where a composer should stand at a rehearsal. After a pause of a couple of seconds, Chris brought the baton down in a firm stroke and the strange wall of sound started.

The opening bars came as a shock. The violins sounded like they came in before the woodwind players, as though they were out of time with each other. Or maybe they were playing a bit faster than the woodwind section, I couldn't tell which. Chris carried on beating time regardless, sweeping his conductor's baton up and down to mark time and the musicians kept glancing at him over the top of their scores, as they skim read the unfamiliar notes.

The thing was, I had a dream about this night. Not a real dream, more of a wishful daydream. And in my daydream, I imagined that the first time the orchestra played my music, it would sound as perfectly formed and passionate as I'd heard it in my head these past few months. That was what I imagined. But here in the room, it sounded uncoordinated and restrained, and I didn't realize that it was often like this when an orchestra played a new, unfamiliar piece for the first time. Instead, I felt my stomach grip in fear as a terrible thought took hold. It was my music that was the problem. Something about my music was wrong.

Then I started thinking that maybe I'd made a terrible mistake, believing I could write proper classical music, and now the orchestra were being forced into playing my music and probably hating it. The stupid, illiterate punk musician who thought he could write a classical symphony.

Eventually, after what felt like an eternity, the third, final movement came to an end and everyone lowered their instruments, and every head in the orchestra turned to look at Chris. There were no smiles, no reactions to the music, nothing, only the sound of pages of sheet music being turned back to the beginning of the score. The silence felt intensely uncomfortable and disappointing, because another hope I had about this moment was that someone would say how much the music moved them, or at the very least, say they enjoyed playing it. But no one did.

Hardly aware that I'd moved, I found myself back at the table in the far corner of the hall and sat down on the edge of it as Chris instructed the orchestra to begin playing the first movement again. By now tired and hungry, I no longer heard what was being played as my disappointment muffled my hearing so that I didn't have to endure the painful experience of listening to my inadequate symphony being performed one more time.

When the rehearsal finally came to an end, I left as fast as I could after saying goodbye to Ian and caught the last bus home. Back at the flat, I looked at the discarded shirts on my bed, the ones I'd tried on earlier.

Idiot, they never even looked at your shirt.

Over the next couple of days, I tried to forget the rehearsal but awkward moments from the evening kept surfacing, and every time the phone rang, I half-expected it to be Chris, calling to say that they were sorry, but they'd realized it was a terrible mistake agreeing to play my symphony in the concert and that they'd made the last-minute decision to replace it with another one, a proper classical piece of music.

Eventually, I calmed down, realizing that if they hated it that much, they would have phoned by now. But no one did, and when the call didn't come, I tried to convince myself that things would be better at the second rehearsal on Friday night, the last one before the premiere.

Three days later, in the same drab, municipal hall, stood at the back of the hall next to Ian, I stared down at my shoes and mentally kicked myself for what had just happened. I'd obviously done the wrong thing again and it was too late to fix it.

"Can the violins open up at the end of the first movement, build the intensity so that the strings really stand out for the last few notes?" I'd said to everyone in the room just before they were about to run through the first movement again. All I wanted was for them to play it with a bit more passion but addressing the orchestra directly just before Chris was about to speak was obviously not the done thing.

"Don't tell the musicians how to play, the performance interpretation should be written down in the score," said Ian quietly.

For a few moments, the pin-drop silence was loud and uncomfortable, just odd creaks of chairs and shuffling of feet.

Finally, after what seemed like ages, Chris spoke as he raised his baton again.

"Right, everyone. Let's take it from bar 54 again and play to the end of the first movement, shall we?"

At the end of the session, when Chris started giving out last minute details about Saturday night's concert and everyone started talking and packing away their instruments, the moment came to quietly escape. As I went out of the door, I heard him announce that the concert was now completely sold out, every ticket gone.

I hurried out into the car park and waited by Ian's car to make sure I was out of sight before any of the musicians left, and within a few minutes, Ian came out and walked over to the car and unlocked it.

"Want a lift, it's on my way?" he offered, his voice sounding relaxed and cheerful, different to how he'd seemed inside.

"Thanks," I replied, grateful to be able to get into his car and out of everyone's sight so that I could gather my thoughts. The final rehearsal felt even worse than the first one, and as the car sped along the dark St. Ives roads towards my flat, I tried to reassure myself that it was just the pressure of the concert building inside my head.

Later, alone in my flat, sat in the dark sitting room with my head in my hands, I realized that everything I'd ever feared had come back to confront me in this situation. Education, knowledge, class, confidence and authority, all so perfectly encapsulated in the inscrutable orchestra, a sea of eyes melded into one critical stare which seemed to say, "How dare you attempt to enter our world. How dare you presume that you can cut out years of classical training, hard-won musical education, background, intelligence, dedication. How dare you presume you can side-step all of that and write classical music and expect us to play it."

I may have gone through a near-death experience, but this

was the stuff of my deepest nightmares, everything I'd ever felt intimidated by, every part of my life coming to a head in that rehearsal room, the pinnacle of everything that had ever weighed down on me, and as I thought about it, my mind started racing with a sense of panic that felt like a swarm of angry bees buzzing inside.

Eventually, feeling cold and tired, I roused myself and looked at my watch. It was after midnight. Exhausted, I shut down the computer and went to bed.

Chapter 23

A Different Drummer

"So, do you want to tell me exactly what happened?" said Irene calmly.

I was sat in the same chair as usual, the comfortable one by her office window.

"I messed up. I looked like a bloody idiot. I can't do this."

"Do what?" she asked in the same calm tone.

"Be the classical composer. I can't do it. I'm..."

"What?"

"Stupid. I can't even read the score, the sheet music. They all look at me like I'm stupid."

"Who does?"

"The orchestra."

"How can you tell they think that? What do they say exactly?"

"They don't say anything," I said, feeling a knot of anger in my stomach. "That's the point. They just look at me."

"So, let me get this straight. You can tell what the musicians in the orchestra are thinking by how they look at you?"

"Yeah, it's obvious."

"Then let me congratulate you on your amazing mind-reading skills. I only wish I had half your ability to read minds, it would make my job so much easier," she said, a half-smile forming on her face.

I sighed and sat back in the chair and tried to calm down enough to explain it more clearly.

"I asked them to play with more intensity at the end of the first movement, build the dynamic. That was all I said. I just wanted them to play it a bit differently."

"And did they?" she asked.

"Well, yeah, they did. But then Ian said I shouldn't tell

the orchestra musicians how to perform the music like that. Apparently, it's all supposed to be written down in the score."

"So basically, you have a lot to learn in this new role?"

"There are all sorts of unwritten rules in classical music. Don't do this. Don't be yourself. Don't show any emotion. Don't react to anything. How am I supposed to know what to do?"

"Has it ever occurred to you that the orchestra musicians might actually be nervous of you? It can't be easy, having the composer stood at the front, watching over you as you learn to play music you've never seen before? Maybe they were wondering what you thought of them? Have you considered that possibility?"

"No... not really."

"It doesn't matter if they are educated or that they can read music and you can't. That doesn't make them into bad people and it certainly doesn't make you bad either. It just means you have a lot to learn, that's all."

"Anyway. It's all arranged now. The concert is sold out. I couldn't back out even if I wanted to."

"Do you want to back out?" she asked, raising her eyebrows.

"Do I have a choice?"

"Yes, you do. You can choose to give up entirely. You could even go back to drinking and sink into self-hatred and let that destroy everything you have built for yourself since your accident. That's an easy route for you. It's so familiar, you've had years of practice of feeling intimidated by people who you believe have power over you, because on a deeper level, you feel they abuse that power. In fact, I'd argue that the orchestra might actually be serving as a stand-in for certain unconscious feelings you transfer onto anyone you perceive to have authority over you."

"What do you mean?"

"From what you've told me over the past few months, the way you've described yourself, it seems to me that deep down, you don't like yourself very much. In fact, it seems to me that you blame yourself for a whole lot of things that have happened in your life and you've blamed yourself for so long, you don't even know you are doing it anymore. But this concert is your chance to become aware of this unconscious feeling, acknowledge where it came from, see it for what it is. An illusion. Nothing more. You are the only person who has power over you and what you think about yourself. Not those people you think are educated, or powerful, or middle class. When you can see the truth of this, you can finally recognize these feelings for what they are, and when you can do that, it offers the possibility of real change."

For some strange reason, a lump appeared in my throat, and Irene must have noticed, because her voice mellowed, as though she'd changed tack to explain something in a softer way.

"Look. I'm going to suggest another way of looking at things. I'm not saying it's the truth, but I want you to consider the possibility. Is that okay with you?"

I nodded, unable to speak.

"It's possible that when you were a child, you wanted your parents' love very badly, but you secretly believed that you were bad or stupid. And because you were only a child, with a child's understanding of life, you had no clear idea how to be clever or good to win their love back. Your biggest fear in life was that your parents would eventually stop loving you altogether if you kept making them unhappy, and because you felt that you weren't worthy of their love but didn't understand why, that made you feel very vulnerable. But what you fail to see is that there never was anything wrong with who you were or how you felt, ever. You were just very sensitive as a child, and because you were so sensitive, you became very aware of other people's reactions and behaviors and you developed some mistaken beliefs in response to what you thought was going on around you. Like the belief that your parents were disappointed and angry with you all the time, when in reality, like many parents, what you saw was probably their struggle with their own insecurities and anxieties in life. Challenges which were nothing to do with who you were or what you were like. Does any of this make sense to you?"

She paused, obviously waiting to see what my reaction was as the impact of her words began to sink in and I felt a long-forgotten tension in my body lessen its grip as she carried on speaking, dissecting further and deeper into an old wound with her kind and steady voice.

"The thing is, you were only a child, so you didn't understand any of this. You just thought you were making them unhappy, so you ended up believing that you were bad, and because you failed at school, that you were stupid too. Eventually, you believed that the only way to get love was to sort out everyone else's problems first and make sure they were happy. Because love had to be earned when you were stupid and bad. You didn't get it for free."

"But my parents did... do love me," I said, the lump in my throat pressing harder now.

"I don't doubt it for one minute," she replied. "But when a parent acts out of need or guilt and unintentionally manipulates their child because of their own unhealed issues, it doesn't mean that they don't love them. It means that they are not loving them in a healthy way at that particular moment. That's hard for a child to understand. In your case, it led you to believe that you were making your parents unhappy, and as a consequence, you've done a good job of beating yourself up ever since. Just like you're doing now, with the orchestra."

I swallowed hard. The strange thing was, somewhere deep inside, I felt like I'd been waiting for someone to say all this for a long time.

"I think it's the same for you with your brother," Irene continued. "You have an image of your brother as the one who's more successful and you see yourself as the failure of the family. Because he's older and more educated, he carries part of that role for you. But you need to let go of that good son, bad son image you carry around, the unfinished business of your relationship with him. Because I think the thing you want so badly from him, his respect, I believe it's already there. It's obvious, by the way he's helped you so much with your music, and yet it's you that has entered into his world, his domain. In a way, it's perfect. The whole situation. Because it offers you a whole new way to experience each other. So, I suggest you make another choice here."

"What's that?" I said, my voice unexpectedly croaky.

"To have some faith in yourself. Do you have any idea just how amazing you really are? I've worked with a lot of patients who have had serious accidents and they don't make the kind of changes you have. If you can make these kinds of changes, you can certainly cope with a group of well-educated, classical musicians. And you can certainly deal with the fact that your brother can read music and you can't."

She chewed her lip for a moment as though deciding whether to say something else, then spoke again, her voice softer now.

"Do you remember when you first told me about your near-death experience, and I said you wouldn't have an easy time, convincing people?"

"You mean people like you?" I said, half-smiling.

"Yes. But, if it's proof you want, maybe you did bring something back. First your paintings and now your music. I've never seen anything like it in all my years of clinical practice. At first, I thought it was probably nothing more than a hallucination. But I've looked into the brain-based theories, the dying brain, the chemical changes of the brain under intense pressure, the activation of NMDA receptors, hypoxia, excess carbon dioxide, temporal lobe epilepsy, but none of these biological processes explain your paintings and your music."

We stared at each other for a moment.

"So, you believe me now?" I asked, taken aback. I was so used to Irene doubting my near-death experience that it came as a shock to hear her admit her own doubts.

"I'll tell you what I believe," she said, taking off her glasses. "A lot of people who claim to be enlightened after a peak spiritual experience deny what's true for them, so they can't move past the unacknowledged stuff from the past because it's all bottled up inside. To me, that's not enlightenment. It's nothing like it. As far as I am concerned, the real path to enlightenment is knowing every part of yourself, going into all the dark corners, all the pain that's hidden away and bringing it out into the light of day. And that's what I'm asking you to do now, to see that your journey has brought you to the most perfect place to confront your deepest fears. It's all there, right in front of you, projected perfectly onto the blank canvas that the orchestra are providing."

"So, what do I do?" I said quietly, avoiding her eyes.

"You draw on what you say you experienced in that other world," she replied. "You acknowledge the unconscious insecurities that are driving your behavior and learn to love yourself in the process, just as you are. Then you go through with the concert and when you sit there on the night, you take a moment to feel proud of yourself. You acknowledge that you've turned your life around because you've found a way to do something with your life that has real meaning. Something that leaves this world a better place than you found it. Not everyone has a chance to do that."

We sat in silence for a few moments as I absorbed her words. The idea of facing the orchestra still made me feel anxious, but I knew she was right. I had been led to this point. Of course I had to go through with it. There never was any other choice.

"Isn't there one more thing you want to talk about before you go?" she said, breaking the silence.

"I can't think of anything?"

"Are you sure?" she said, looking at me in a curious way.

"Well... I'm thinking of asking Anna to the concert."

"That's good, isn't it?"

"Maybe. I don't know."

"Listen to me, David. Your art, your music, it's wonderful. But it's all you are doing. It has taken over your life. It's as though you feel it's your only consolation in the absence of a relationship."

"I can't help feeling compelled to write music and paint—"

"I'm not saying it's wrong," she cut in, leaning forward. "All I am saying is, your art and your music should support your life, not the other way around. It's not enough in life to be just a wonderful artist, it's essential to be ordinary and to find yourself in the ordinary. There is no lasting fulfilment in greatness, the lasting fulfilment is in the ordinary. That's where you will find real love."

"But outside of my painting, my music, my near-death experience, I don't know who I am," I finally admitted, as much to myself as to Irene.

"You are a kind, compassionate, warm human being, but until you commit to love, your life won't be truly complete," she replied. "We think of love in sentimental terms, but it's not. Real love is a verb. It's something that has to flow, it needs to move, flow out of us in order to come into existence and it has to have a destination that's bigger than us. If you experienced unconditional love in that other world, then you need to really think about what unconditional love means in this life as well. When I look around me, I see glimpses of it in all kinds of situations. It's there, if you just know where to look."

"I don't think anyone could love me like that."

"Someone might, if you give them the chance. But then of course you would need to love them back in the same way, even if they did squeeze the toothpaste from the middle of the tube or do all the things that might drive you up the wall. Do you think you could do that?"

"I'm not sure I know how to open up..."

"I'll tell you how you can," she said, smiling. "You keep on connecting to your heart. You continue this journey you are on, you feel all the old pain, all the sadness that's there and you honor it, because it's your truth. And if you do, there is a very good chance that underneath all that, you might find something else."

"What?"

"Your true feelings for Anna."

At that moment, the digital clock beeped to say the session was over. I started to get to my feet, but she raised her hand to signal me to stop, her brow furrowed as she looked like she was trying to remember something. Then her expression relaxed as she found it.

"The philosopher Henry David Thoreau wrote some wise words about a man who takes his own path in life," she said, smiling again. "I think of you when I hear them."

When she said Thoreau's words out loud, they made me think of me too.

Chapter 24

What Will Survive of Us is Love

The dream is going well. You are with your brother, you are both at the Pleasure Beach funfair in Blackpool, on the flying cage ride. You have a cage each on the ride, like you always do on holiday here. You look across at him. He looks a lot younger, like you remember he looked before he got serious. You say to him, "How high can you swing?" and he says, "Higher than you," and you both laugh and you both start swinging your cages back and forth, swinging higher and higher until you can't swing anymore for laughing.

You laugh so much that you have to take in deep breaths and your arms are sore. Then you both stop swinging and you talk and he listens and you tell him things you know he'll understand because he's older. Then he reaches across and puts his arm around your shoulder and he makes you feel that everything will be okay after all. You say to him, "I miss this," and he says, "Me too," and you see how much love there is between you and you ask him how you can both come back to this place. And as the dream begins to fade, you remember he tells you not to worry, it will always be there...

I sat on the sofa in the living room, continuously yawning, my hands around a mug of coffee as one daytime program after another blared out of the television. I thought about tonight's concert, and for the hundredth time, kicked myself. Why was it so hard to call Anna? But Irene was right. I had to try.

As the lunchtime television news started, I reached across to pick up my mobile, scrolled through the contacts list to find her number, tapped on it, then held the phone to my ear. I had no idea what I was going to say, but the decision had been made to call her at long last.

I kept watching the television screen as I listened to the ringing tone, and at first, only half-focused on the banner that ran across the bottom of the screen, identifying the BBC Television reporter who was speaking to the camera. But then, images of Huntingdon station suddenly appeared on the screen and I quickly reached for the remote and turned the sound up to listen.

"His accident was a life-changing event," I heard her say. "David Ditchfield was horrifically injured when his coat was caught in the doors of a train and he was dragged under the wheels as it pulled away. But remarkably, he didn't die, and as he lay critically injured in hospital, he said he had a near-death experience, where he met Beings of Light and felt himself surrounded by unconditional love and acceptance. This experience changed his life and gave him a new meaning and purpose and inspired him to write a classical symphony, called *The Divine Light*, which is being premiered tonight here in St. Ives."

Then the images on screen changed in quick succession. First, a shot of tonight's concert venue, then the tenor singer Julian appeared in close-up, as a banner across the bottom of the screen identified him as the Choral Society Conductor and Leader, and his familiar voice came out of the television speaker, responding to questions from an off-screen reporter who was interviewing him.

"With *The Divine Light*, David has composed a piece of music in a completely different voice to any music he would have known before his accident and it is remarkable to see how accomplished he is able to be with this."

Finally, a shot of the orchestra rehearsing and a close-up of *The Divine Light* score appeared on screen as the female reporter's voice concluded the news item, saying, "*The Divine Light* will be performed by the St. Ives Chamber orchestra tonight. It's a poignant piece and follows in the footsteps of other great composers."

Anna sighed. "You could have called before? You had my number?" She sounded like she was half-teasing, but I couldn't be sure as I could only hear her voice, I couldn't see her face.

"I'm really sorry, I needed to sort a few things out first."

"That's a pretty lame excuse."

"I know, I am sorry, honestly."

"Anyway, it's been ages and it's a bit short notice, calling me up on the day."

"I know," I said, hoping against hope that she hadn't got anything else planned for this evening. "But will you come if you can? I'd really like you to be there, it's the premiere tonight and you are such an important part of all this."

"Maybe. I'll see."

I felt a glimmer of hope as her tone sounded warmer now. "I'll leave your name on the door then," I said. "Just tell them you're my guest."

"If I come..."

"If you come."

As night fell, I had to admit, it was a beautiful summer's evening. I couldn't have asked for a more perfect night for the concert. The sky was a deepening blue and the moon was beginning to rise above St. Ives when we arrived at the venue. I looked at Janet, Charlie and my parents getting out of the car and paused for a moment to take in what was actually happening in my life right now. It was a different world entirely and I wanted to remember every moment of this night forever.

As a family group, we walked past the queue of people outside and headed into the building. That was one small advantage of being the composer, I didn't have to queue to get into my own concert. Ian was already inside setting up his French horn, I explained to Mum and Dad, as we shuffled past the busy ticket desk.

The concert was being held in the largest church in St. Ives. A beautiful stone building, dating back to medieval times with a huge stained-glass window at the far end. Janet said the church used to have rows of long wooden pews, but they were removed many years ago and replaced with lighter, portable folding chairs which could easily be stacked when not in use.

Tonight, it looked like every folding chair in the building had been set out and the tightly-packed rows went right to the back of the room. The place was already three-quarters full and the room was buzzing with conversation.

Joy and some of the other healers from the Spiritual Church were sat together in two rows near the back. They all looked over as we made our way up the crowded central aisle towards the front of the room, and I waved and smiled, and they all waved back. Irene was sat a few rows in front and she smiled and waved too as I walked past, and from somewhere deep inside, I felt a wave of deep affection and gratitude seeing both women here, supporting me at my first concert.

A few rows further up on the other side, I spotted Jimmy and Matt, looking very out of place and both wearing a tie and jacket of some description. I'd never seen either of them dressed up before and it took me a moment to recognize them.

Matt's jacket looked slightly too big for him, like he'd borrowed it from someone heavier, and when I managed to make my way along the row of already-seated people to speak to them, the tie had an unmistakable stain that was definitely not part of the pattern, but I was touched they'd both made the effort and said so.

Jimmy smiled when I said that, but Matt seemed quieter than normal. In fact, if I had to put my finger on it, I'd say he seemed a bit intimidated by so many well-behaved people in the audience. I'd never seen him like this before. He even lowered his voice a bit when he spoke.

"You're moving up in the world, mate. It's sold out."

"Did you get the guest tickets? I left them on the door for you?"

"Yeah. Although they gave us the once-over before they let us in," he said, looking slightly sheepish.

"Probably thought you were out to strip the lead roof," I said, grinning. Jimmy grinned too, then chewed his lip, like he was going to say something important. And as a matter of fact, he did.

"Er... got something to tell you."

"What?" I asked.

"I've met someone," he said, bashfully. "I would have brought her along tonight, only I wasn't sure she'd get in, what with it being sold out an' all."

"You should have brought her. Where did you meet?"

"At the Shoreditch party. The one I invited you to. It'd be perfect except for the fact that this dumb idiot here pulled her best friend as well," he said, jerking his head in Matt's direction. "Means we have to go out on double dates all the time."

"And what's wrong with that?" said Matt, indignantly.

"Nothing, except for having to sit opposite you when you're trying to be romantic makes me wanna throw up," said Jimmy, pulling a mock expression of disgust.

"She likes me," retorted Matt. "She said so."

"I reckon she feels sorry for you more like," retorted Jimmy.

Matt put his two fingers up at Jimmy, then realized where he was and quickly put his hands down into his jacket pocket, and Jimmy rolled his eyes and shook his head, but they both looked happier than I'd seen them in ages.

As I made my way back along the row to the main aisle, I had to laugh as I looked back and saw two very large, very stern-looking women squeeze in the two empty seats next to Matt, and my last sight of him was when he disappeared behind a wall of tweed twin-sets, pearls and large, sturdy leather handbags.

Our seats had been reserved on the front row, right next to

the two stone steps which led up to the chancel. I knew it was called the chancel because I'd picked up a leaflet at the front door which had a helpful diagram of the church architecture in it. The orchestra chairs and music stands were laid out in sweeping semicircles under the high domed chancel ceiling, overlooked by a huge stained-glass window in the apex and two large, clear-glass windows on either side.

By the time we sat down, several of the orchestra musicians were already in their seats, getting instruments out of cases and putting their scores out onto their music stands. They looked very formal, the men in their black eveningwear and the women in long, black evening dresses. I could hear the sound of instruments being tuned and musicians talking to one another, and as I looked around, I could see Ian sat in the horn section, fixing his mouthpiece to his French horn.

The conductor's podium had been placed at the front of the orchestra, and Chris was talking to several people who were gathered round him. *The Divine Light* score was poking out of his leather briefcase, and that was when the anxiety started to rise up inside, and that was when I exhaled deeply and reminded myself that the music wasn't just down to me. I had been helped. The same with the paintings. I had to trust that I wouldn't have been guided to this moment if it wasn't meant to be happening.

I took some deeper, steadying breaths and managed to calm myself again, and began to look at the concert program. At least that way I could hide how anxious I was feeling, or so I thought.

"You seem really tense," whispered Janet placing her hand very gently on my forearm. She was right, the concert program was shaking in my hands. Then she reached into her bag, pulled out a small white envelope and handed it to me.

"What's this?" I asked, turning it over in my hand.

"Open it and see," she said.

Inside the envelope was a small home-made card, and as soon as I looked at the picture on the front, I knew it was hand-painted: the small, thin brush strokes, the care with which the color and reflection of everything had been perfectly captured, the dark tones and complementary colors of the Great Ouse riverbank contrasting beautifully with the soft luminescence of the natural daylight on the flowing water, and I spotted the small signature at the bottom as I opened the card to read the handwritten message inside.

To David. Good luck for tonight. We are all so proud of you, love Janet, Charlie and the boys xxx

"Thought you might like one of my paintings," she said, smiling, "after all, it's you that inspired me to start."

I was so moved, I could barely get the words of thanks out, and still holding the card tightly in my hand, I looked up at the side window of the chancel to stop myself from feeling any more emotional than I already was.

It was getting darker outside, and as I gazed out through the plain glass to the evening sky, a white dove fluttered out of nowhere and landed silently on the stone windowsill. It was still perched there twenty minutes later, by which time the entire orchestra had taken their seats, opened their scores and tuned their instruments.

All the lights above the audience suddenly dimmed, so that only the orchestra area was illuminated by a row of intense spotlights. The audience chatter became a quiet hush. Chris walked up to the conductor's podium, and in a clear, confident voice addressed the audience, welcoming everyone to the concert and introducing the evening's program, but I didn't hear any of it; I was too nervous to focus on what he was saying. Then, after he'd finished speaking, he turned back to face the orchestra, picked up his baton and every member of the orchestra raised their instruments ready to play, watching him intently.

For a moment, there was complete silence. In the silence, the air itself was alive and crackling with the electric atmosphere of the crowded room. Then, without a word, Chris raised his baton high in the air and paused for a moment, and the hairs on the back of my neck rose up. After all the months and months of hard work, the moment had arrived. This was it. They were about to begin, and as he swept his baton downwards, cutting through the air, everyone started to play.

The opening strings of the first movement drifted up into the high apex roof, and I listened intently to each note as it left the instrument that had created it and resonated out into the atmosphere of the packed church. And as the first and second movements were played, I found myself back there, in the World of Light, and I felt an overwhelming sense of being at one with an absolute, total, unconditional and all-encompassing love, as though I was part of the one universal source of all life.

I knew it, just like the Apollo astronauts who made it into space and dreamed amongst the stars knew it. There is no separation, we are all as one.

At the end of the second movement, I glanced across at the window. The dove was still perched there. Silent. Watching. Then, out of the corner of my eye, I saw Julian, the tenor singer, get up from his seat. The final movement had started, and I'd almost forgotten that he was sat quietly at the side of the chancel, waiting in the wings. He walked to the front of the orchestra and readied himself to begin. He took a few slow, deep breaths, in the way that professional singers do, and when he opened his mouth and his voice soared and filled the air throughout the room, I felt overwhelmed with the beauty of it. I'd forgotten that I'd written the words all those months ago on Heacham beach under the starlight and the meteors. Instead, like everyone else in the room, I sat transfixed as he sang.

It was a strange feeling, moment by moment, knowing the movement of every note and phrase, knowing exactly what was coming next, every part played perfectly, each section in the orchestra playing as one. Eventually, the final movement reached its climax and as the last notes of the symphony rang out in the huge church for what seemed like an eternity, I looked up at the white dove, still sat outside on the stone ledge of the window, until eventually, the notes faded into a powerful, electric silence. Pin-drop type of silence.

Everyone in the orchestra was still for a moment, then instruments were slowly lowered and shoulders dropped as if the players were coming out of a trance. Chris lowered his arms and placed his rosewood baton on the old wooden podium. It was so silent in the room that I could even hear the slight click his baton made as he put it down. And then, suddenly, a loud, roaring noise rose up in my ear.

People began clapping. The clapping grew louder and louder, like a wave of thunder filling the church. The air was filled with clapping and then I heard cheers and whistles too.

"Bravo."

"Well done."

I looked at the orchestra, and felt so grateful and full of respect for their moving performance. They had played *The Divine Light* brilliantly. Several of the musicians looked over at me and their smiles seemed really genuine, which confirmed that Irene had been right all along. Now it was all over, I could see everything in a better, clearer perspective.

As the wild clapping continued, I searched amongst the faces in the orchestra to find my brother's face. He was beaming and it was so great to see him smiling like that. His smile meant that I'd done something good, and at that moment, I decided it was okay. It was enough. I didn't need him to believe my story. It didn't really matter whether he did or not. What mattered was that he'd helped me when I asked him to. That was what counted. That was what real love was. And it felt really good. And I loved him very much too.

Janet nudged me, but I barely noticed.

Then she nudged me again. More urgently this time.

"David. Look. Look behind you. Look. LOOK."

I turned around and looked.

Everyone in the room was standing. The noise of the clapping was tremendous now, and people were cheering and whistling. The hairs on the back of my neck stood up and tears welled up in my eyes as the cheers and clapping intensified, and I realized that people were clapping me as much as the orchestra. Through all the darkness, I never imagined a day like this would come, and now it had, I'd never felt more humbled in all my life.

And then I saw her, stood at the back of the church. Clapping with all her heart and smiling so beautifully. It was all I could do to not run up and grab her there and then, but she started making her way through the crowd towards me, and as she did, in my heart I prayed that she would believe in the best in me. That she would hold me to it, even if I failed, that she would still keep believing in me and know that I could do it for her, and that what I did for her mattered. That she would let me be a brave and courageous man for her, giving to her in whatever way I could. And I hoped that she would believe I was noble too, a man who would be strong with the world and gentle with those he loves.

This is what I hoped, and this was when I knew, I didn't have to feel afraid of love. I just knew it, like I knew how to breathe. Everything Irene and Joy had said about love now made sense. Only when you have found yourself and can be yourself with another are you worthy of it.

At that very moment, the dove gracefully and silently rose up from the sill, stretched its wings and flew upwards, disappearing into the velvet of the beautiful night sky as I understood the absolute truth of my near-death experience and my journey to this moment. In the vastness of everything, in the journey of our life, the one thing that makes it bearable, is love.

Appendix: The Real-Life Witnesses

Interview with Sarah Asbury, Former Occupational Therapist, NHS Cambridgeshire, Addenbrooke's Hospital

J.S. Jones: *"As part of the medical team treating David at Addenbrooke's Hospital, did you notice anything unusual or different about David compared to other trauma patients?"*

Sarah Asbury: "Yes, I did. There was something very, very significant about David, he was very different from the other patients right from the start. It was about a month into the treatment period after his accident when he told me about his near-death experience, and the more time I spent with David, the more I realized this is what he experienced. This is the reality of what he experienced, and I had 100% respect for it. I know full well that what he experienced was what he experienced. At no point did I ever doubt or question his account. His art, his music, it just speaks volumes in itself. Experiences like David's have made me think that death is not so frightening; there is good stuff there. I haven't come across any other patient that reported such an experience. It has certainly enriched his life and made him live his life in such a positive way."

Interview with Janet, David's sister

J.S. Jones: *"As David's sister, did he seem different to you after his near-death experience?"*

Janet: "The near-death experience and everything that went with that became more apparent after he was discharged from hospital. Then, he was very talkative about it all, researching different things, talking about it an awful lot. I'd say he was consumed by it, he really was, he was really bright from it all, so uplifted. It had a major positive effect on him, and I am sure it helped him through those hard days when he was recovering from his injuries. It has clearly changed his life forever, hugely. If you can imagine from how dark his life was before the accident, then his life-threatening, rare shocking accident, then to David's whole brightness from his near-death experience when he came home. It was really bonkers, it honestly was."

Interview with Derek and Margaret, David's parents

J.S. Jones: *"What do you both think about David's near-death experience? Do you believe it really happened?"*

Margaret: "When he told us, he was so full of it. I do believe it was something mystical. His face was very alight when he told us. There was something about his face that was very bright. He changed a lot after his experience, and he was so anxious to do the painting of it. I remember he even tried to get the nurses to help him draw it. He was very determined that he wanted to get it down on paper, that was how he was."

Derek: "The near-death experience was such a meaningful thing to David, it was a spiritual adventure. He changed a lot after it. Especially spiritually, there was a definite change there. Despite the terrible accident, his mind seemed quite content and calm afterwards, accepting everything that had happened to him."

J.S. Jones: *"Were you surprised at your son's sudden ability to compose classical music after his near-death experience?"*

Margaret: "I was taken aback; I was shocked when he composed his symphony. When we went to the premiere, the symphony was so very moving. His ability to compose classical music has grown since. We both feel he has done so well because he had no training in how to write this type of music at all, no training in how to put it down."

J.S. Jones: *"Has David's experience changed your views about life* *after death?"*

Derek: "It's definitely made my faith more secure about what could happen in the afterlife."

Margaret: "I feel the same. They don't talk about the afterlife in the church service. It's surprising how people, really religious people, don't always believe there is anything. That is strange really, because that is what Easter is all about, and that is when it does come to the fore, when people start thinking about things like that. At church, it's not really discussed at all. But if there is life after death, where do we go? It must be to some other place, like the one David went to. That's a lovely thought to hold on to."

Interview with Richard McDonnell, President of the St. Ives Spiritualist Church

J.S. Jones: *"You were at the premiere of David's NDE-inspired symphony,* The Divine Light. *What was that evening like for you?"*

Richard: "We all wanted to be there, all the healers, everyone who knew David from the Spiritual Church wanted to be there at the premiere, so we booked out the back two rows of seats.

It was such a wonderful night; the music was so beautiful. Because we knew about his NDE, you could feel exactly which part of his NDE was represented by each bit of music. It was so moving. The whole evening stayed with me, it was so special, even now I can recall it.

I think people that have had an NDE, they come back differently, it changes their lives once they take a glimpse at what's ahead of us; they come back blessed because they know that one day we will all reach the Spirit World and experience that wonderful reunion with loved ones. I think David has definitely made this transition and has come back for a reason. What he has received is a marvelous, marvelous gift. His paintings of his NDE, his music, it's all stayed with me and he has been such an influence on people that know his story. Even now, people still come into the church and ask about him. The speed of his recovery, the way he came on so quickly, it's so amazing."

Interview with Richard and Jane Waters, Time for Health Pilates Yoga Studio, St. Ives

J.S. Jones: *"David painted a number of his NDE paintings in the attic of your Yoga studio. How did this come about?"*

Richard: "We bumped into David quite by chance one day. He was walking past the yoga studios carrying his sketchbook and Jane happened to walk out the front door." Jane:

"We'd already heard about his accident and we got chatting and he said he was looking for an art studio. As our building was closed for repairs for one week, we offered him the use of the attic space as a temporary studio and a trestle table to paint on. He had a huge blank canvas at the time but nowhere big enough to set it up to paint on. There was a real synchronicity to the whole situation, how I bumped into him just when he was looking for somewhere to paint. That's what really struck me at the time, the synchronicity of it all, it felt stranger than I can describe."

Richard: "As soon as he started painting, we could see he was really onto something and it was great having him around doing his art, so it became an open-ended invitation. It was a really good energy, people seemed to be popping in and out asking if they could go up to see David and look at his paintings. It became like a little community of interested people who wanted to see how he was progressing and how the paintings were coming on. In the end, he did so many paintings in our attic, we ended up telling everyone he was our artist-in-residence. It was wonderful to be a part of it."

J.S. Jones, PhD, co-author of *Shine On*

These events happened and I was a part of them. Having witnessed David's story firsthand, I believe it is a remarkable tale that deserves to be told. David has profound dyslexia, so I was delighted when he asked me to co-author the book because he felt I was the one person who could understand his thought processes and capture his language, mood and emotions to help tell his story as authentically as possible. From my own creative perspective, my long-standing friendship with him offered me a vantage point to not only critically verify the profound changes he has gone through firsthand, but to also draw out and expand on the greater life-enhancing themes embedded in his story. It also allowed me access to interview his family and friends involved in the key events, from a place of friendship and trust.

In a strange way, throughout the writing process, *Shine On* has felt like there has been something greater hidden in the mystery of its journey, from its first draft to the final published book. Not only has the writing process constantly reminded me to make a deeper connection to my own inner nature, but it has also felt like a spiritual journey in its own right, mysteriously connected to some wider purpose that *Shine On* is meant to be a small part of. Perhaps it is to do with a natural yearning in all of us to connect with the magical place David describes in his near-death experience, and the hope and comfort of hearing from someone who has seen 'the other side' for themselves, firsthand, that it is all there waiting for us and for that, I remain eternally grateful.

The Divine Light Symphony Notes

1st Movement: *Adagio*

The first movement describes the powerful transition David goes through, journeying to another world as the emergency department doctors fight to save him. From the opening notes, his music aims to give the listener an experience of what this serene and calm other-world feels like, with the powerful crescendo of strings, brass and timpani representing the moment he becomes aware of the Androgynous Being of Light and feels an overwhelming sense of unconditional love emanating from its presence.

2nd Movement

The second movement evokes a sense of a powerful awakening to the love that surrounds him, the rhythmic frame of the trumpet, cellos and strings representing the impact of this intense rush of awareness resonating in every cell of his body. A crescendo of timpani, cymbals and strings transforms into a tender refrain, carried by the strings and woodwind, reflecting the sense of wonder he experiences in this eternal moment as a voice inside his head whispers, "You are safe, everything is well. You are loved."

3rd Movement

The third movement describes his peak experience of seeing a great luminous, brilliant tunnel of radiant light, swirling at his feet, as he realises this is the Source of all life itself, and the tenor vocal part embodies the overwhelming feeling of peace David feels in its presence. This is the moment he understands the meaning and purpose of his experience. In the vastness of everything, in the journey of our life, the one thing that makes it bearable, is love.

About the Authors

David Ditchfield

David was born in Blackpool. He left school with only one qualification and then did a course learning how to draw letters for adverts, not a great career choice for someone with profound dyslexia. After being sacked from his one and only 'proper' job, he played guitar in various punk and pop bands and co-wrote a pop song with Kevin Rowlands. Eventually, he drifted away from playing in bands and things went on a downward spiral and he ended up surviving as a manual laborer, his life empty and directionless. His near-death experience (NDE) changed everything and inspired him to reach a level of musical and artistic creativity that he had never achieved before, born out of a desire to reassure everyone that there is nothing to fear after death. Since his NDE, he has completed over 30 paintings and has been commissioned by two classical ensembles to compose a further symphony and rhapsody, both of which have now been premiered at sell-out performances. He is currently working on a new symphony entitled, *I wasn't Expecting This*, and lives, paints and composes in a converted riverside mill near Cambridge, UK.

You can see some of David's NDE-inspired paintings and hear excerpts from his music at: www.shineonthestory.com

And follow him on Instagram:
www.instagram.com/david_ditchfield/

J.S. Jones, PhD

J.S. Jones is a published academic after receiving a PhD from the University of Stirling. Having completed a number of creative writing courses to co-author *Shine On*, J.S. Jones is now working on a debut fiction novel, the first in a planned series and thoroughly enjoying the process.

A Message from David

Thank you for purchasing *Shine On*. Our sincere hope is that you derived as much from reading this story as I had in living the life of it. If you have a few moments, it would be great if you could add your review of the book at your favorite online site for feedback. Also, if you would like to connect with events I have coming in the near future, please visit the *Shine On* website for news on upcoming works and performances.

www.shineonthestory.com
Best wishes,
David

Acknowledgements

Many people have helped in the *Shine On* journey, and deserve acknowledgement and thanks for this. First, Margaret and Derek Ditchfield and Alan Jones (with Joyce always there in the background). Then Janet and Charlie (and the boys), who played such a key role in this story. Special mention must also go to Ian, whose generous help and brotherly support enabled *The Divine Light* symphony to make it to its premiere performance, Ruadhri Cushnan for making the recording happen and Chris Hiscock, Julian Merson, Felicity Wrenwood, Gillian Atherton and the sublime Chamber Orchestra of St. Ives for performing it so beautifully on the night.

Also, grateful thanks go to the wonderful Joy and Irene, whose strength, wisdom and insights fill every page of this book. Also, Richard and Jane Waters, whose generous and unconditional loan of their attic space allowed the NDE paintings to happen.

For the writing, Vera and Jack Sylvester's loving legacy meant that there was a laptop to type this book on and Alan generously provided the log cabin in which to type it.

Additional people to thank include the wonderful Joy and Kenny Foubister, all the amazing healers at the St. Ives Spiritualist Church and the outstanding team at Addenbrooke's Hospital, especially consultant surgeon Mr. Ian Grant, Sarah Asbury, the Occupational Therapist and all the courageous and dedicated nurses who work there.

Finally, thanks go to Stella Webster for being the very first person to read *Shine On* and suggest that it was good enough to get published, D.J. Kermode for her invaluable feedback on the first draft, and last but not least, the lovely Lisa Smartt and the wonderful Dr. Raymond A. Moody, whose enthusiasm and encouragement made all the difference.

BOOKS

SPIRITUALITY

O is a symbol of the world, of oneness and unity; this eye represents knowledge and insight. We publish titles on general spirituality and living a spiritual life. We aim to inform and help you on your own journey in this life.

If you have enjoyed this book, why not tell other readers by posting a review on your preferred book site? Recent bestsellers from O-Books are:

Heart of Tantric Sex
Diana Richardson
Revealing Eastern secrets of deep love and intimacy to Western couples.
Paperback: 978-1-90381-637-0 ebook: 978-1-84694-637-0

Crystal Prescriptions
The A-Z guide to over 1,200 symptoms and their healing crystals
Judy Hall
The first in the popular series of six books, this handy little guide is packed as tight as a pill-bottle with crystal remedies for ailments.
Paperback: 978-1-90504-740-6 ebook: 978-1-84694-629-5

Take Me To Truth
Undoing the Ego
Nouk Sanchez, Tomas Vieira
The best-selling step-by-step book on shedding the Ego, using the
teachings of *A Course In Miracles*.
Paperback: 978-1-84694-050-7 ebook: 978-1-84694-654-7

The 7 Myths about Love...Actually!
The journey from your HEAD to the HEART of your SOUL
Mike George
Smashes all the myths about LOVE.
Paperback: 978-1-84694-288-4 ebook: 978-1-84694-682-0

The Holy Spirit's Interpretation of the New Testament
A Course in Understanding and Acceptance
Regina Dawn Akers
Following on from the strength of *A Course In Miracles*, NTI
teaches us how to experience the love and oneness of God.
Paperback: 978-1-84694-085-9 ebook: 978-1-78099-083-5

The Message of A Course In Miracles
A translation of the Text in plain language
Elizabeth A. Cronkhite
A translation of *A Course in Miracles* into plain, everyday
language for anyone seeking inner peace. The companion
volume, *Practicing A Course In Miracles*, offers practical lessons
and mentoring.
Paperback: 978-1-84694-319-5 ebook: 978-1-84694-642-4

Rising in Love

My Wild and Crazy Ride to Here and Now, with Amma, the
Hugging Saint
Ram Das Batchelder
Rising in Love conveys an author's extraordinary journey of
spiritual awakening with the Guru, Amma.
Paperback: 978-1-78279-687-9 ebook: 978-1-78279-686-2

Thinker's Guide to God

Peter Vardy
An introduction to key issues in the philosophy of religion.
Paperback: 978-1-90381-622-6

Your Simple Path

Find Happiness in every step
Ian Tucker
A guide to helping us reconnect with what is really important in
our lives.
Paperback: 978-1-78279-349-6 ebook: 978-1-78279-348-9

365 Days of Wisdom

Daily Messages To Inspire You Through The Year
Dadi Janki
Daily messages which cool the mind, warm the heart and guide
you along your journey.
Paperback: 978-1-84694-863-3 ebook: 978-1-84694-864-0

Body of Wisdom

Women's Spiritual Power and How it Serves
Hilary Hart
Bringing together the dreams and experiences of women across
the world with today's most visionary spiritual teachers.
Paperback: 978-1-78099-696-7 ebook: 978-1-78099-695-0

Dying to Be Free
From Enforced Secrecy to Near Death to True Transformation
Hannah Robinson
After an unexpected accident and near-death experience, Hannah Robinson found herself radically transforming her life, while a remarkable new insight altered her relationship with her father, a practising Catholic priest.
Paperback: 978-1-78535-254-6 ebook: 978-1-78535-255-3

The Ecology of the Soul
A Manual of Peace, Power and Personal Growth for Real People in the Real World
Aidan Walker
Balance your own inner Ecology of the Soul to regain your natural state of peace, power and wellbeing.
Paperback: 978-1-78279-850-7 ebook: 978-1-78279-849-1

Not I, Not other than I
The Life and Teachings of Russel Williams
Steve Taylor, Russel Williams
The miraculous life and inspiring teachings of one of the World's greatest living Sages.
Paperback: 978-1-78279-729-6 ebook: 978-1-78279-728-9

On the Other Side of Love
A Woman's Unconventional Journey Towards Wisdom
Muriel Maufroy
When life has lost all meaning, what do you do?
Paperback: 978-1-78535-281-2 ebook: 978-1-78535-282-9

Practicing A Course In Miracles
A translation of the Workbook in plain language, with mentor's notes
Elizabeth A. Cronkhite
The practical second and third volumes of The Plain-Language *A Course In Miracles*.
Paperback: 978-1-84694-403-1 ebook: 978-1-78099-072-9

Quantum Bliss
The Quantum Mechanics of Happiness, Abundance, and Health
George S. Mentz
Quantum Bliss is the breakthrough summary of success and spirituality secrets that customers have been waiting for.
Paperback: 978-1-78535-203-4 ebook: 978-1-78535-204-1

The Upside Down Mountain
Mags MacKean
A must-read for anyone weary of chasing success and happiness – one woman's inspirational journey swapping the uphill slog for the downhill slope.
Paperback: 978-1-78535-171-6 ebook: 978-1-78535-172-3

Your Personal Tuning Fork
The Endocrine System
Deborah Bates
Discover your body's health secret, the endocrine system, and 'twang' your way to sustainable health!
Paperback: 978-1-84694-503-8 ebook: 978-1-78099-697-4

Readers of ebooks can buy or view any of these bestsellers by clicking on the live link in the title. Most titles are published in paperback and as an ebook. Paperbacks are available in traditional bookshops. Both print and ebook formats are available online.

Find more titles and sign up to our readers' newsletter at http://www.johnhuntpublishing.com/mind-body-spirit

Follow us on Facebook at https://www.facebook.com/OBooks/ and Twitter at https://twitter.com/obooks